Arland J. Hultgren

18 April, 1988

A PRIMER ON
PRAYER

Contributors

LUTHER NORTHWESTERN
THEOLOGICAL SEMINARY

Terence E. Fretheim
Dean of Academic Affairs, Professor of Old Testament

Frederick J. Gaiser
Dean of Students, Associate Professor of Old Testament

Loren E. Halvorson
John L. Rothrock Professor of Pastoral Theology and Ministry,
Church and Society

Arland J. Hultgren
Professor of New Testament

Eugene C. Kreider
Professor of Pastoral Theology and Ministry, Christian Education

Paul Varo Martinson
Professor of Christian Missions and World Religions

Paul G. Sonnack
Secretary of Faculty, Professor of Church History

Paul R. Sponheim
Professor of Systematic Theology

David L. Tiede
President, Professor of New Testament

Carl A. Volz
Professor of Church History

A PRIMER ON PRAYER

Edited by
Paul R. Sponheim

FORTRESS PRESS
PHILADELPHIA

COPYRIGHT © 1988 BY FORTRESS PRESS

Library of Congress Cataloging-in-Publication Data

A Primer on prayer.

Bibliography: p.
1. Prayer.   I. Sponheim, Paul R.
BV205.P75   1988   248.3'2   87-45903
ISBN 0-8006-2083-6

3222H87   Printed in the United States of America   1-2083

Contents

Preface   vii

Introduction   1

PART ONE.   The Heritage of Prayer

1. Individual and Corporate Prayer in Old
    Testament Perspective   9
    Frederick J. Gaiser

2. Expectations of Prayer in the New Testament   23
    Arland J. Hultgren

3. Prayer in the Early Church   36
    Carl A. Volz

PART TWO.   Understanding Prayer

4. Prayer in the Old Testament: Creating
    Space in the World for God   51
    Terence E. Fretheim

5. The God of Prayer   63
    Paul R. Sponheim

6. People Other Than Christians Pray   77
    Paul Varo Martinson

7. Prayer and Action   91
    Loren E. Halvorson

PART THREE.   The Practice of Prayer

8. The Kingdom Prayer   107
      David L. Tiede

9. Prayer in Public Life   121
      Paul G. Sonnack

10. Learning and Teaching Prayer   135
       Eugene C. Kreider

Epilogue   147

Selected Bibliography   151

Preface

Theological work needs to be done in direct relationship to the actual life of Christians.

The several disciplines of theology need to be kept in close relationship to one another.

These two convictions inform much of the activity at Luther Northwestern Theological Seminary. They were decisive in the formation of the particular stream of activity that was the prayer colloquium, an interdisciplinary project of faculty members organized in the fall of 1984, out of which the essays in this volume were produced.

Prayer is a fitting subject of study for persons holding the two convictions mentioned. As the original proposal for the colloquium put it, the practice of prayer is an indisputable Christian reality. Moreover, we discovered quickly that we would suffer from no dearth of personal questions and theological issues in this work. This was not a matter of casual preference. How we pray and what we believe, what we pray and how we believe—these are not to be disjoined for persons who believe in a God who is one!

With regard to the second conviction, it is clear that prayer is not the private possession of any particular discipline. Biblical studies, church history, systematic theology, missiology, pastoral theology—all these fields can speak to this subject and need to do so. We believe that we have made a beginning in these years of prayer and study. We are glad now to broaden the conversation by presenting material to readers outside the Luther Northwestern community. Thus we reach a third stage in our work. We began by working on these matters over a period of two years, with the understanding that we were speaking directly and personally within the boundaries of the ten of us. Then a year was spent sharing essays with the community, receiving critique and comment from students and faculty. We believe it is now time to continue the process through publication.

We are grateful to the Aid Association for Lutherans for financial assistance throughout the three years of the project. We have never had reason to doubt the support of the seminary administration as well. Harold Rast, Thelma Megill-Cobbler, and Davis Perkins, all of Fortress Press, have assisted us significantly. I am particularly grateful to Arland Hultgren for help in the editorial process. I want to thank my nine colleagues for an extremely stimulating and instructive time together. Together we have sensed the keen interest of a great many people in this project. Perhaps that should not be surprising. Christians pray and think about prayer. Therefore this volume, though only a primer, may stimulate further reflection on prayer in the life of the church. We also hope it will encourage and enhance the practice of prayer.

PAUL R. SPONHEIM

INTRODUCTION

Why pray? Why study prayer? We pray because we need God. We believe that prayer brings us more intimately and fully into contact with God. We believe that through the study of prayer we may come to pray more faithfully and more fruitfully.

Of course one might well answer differently. One might say that one prays out of obedience, habit, or desire. Such answers do illumine aspects of the reality of Christian praying. But most fundamentally, we pray out of our need for God. We may define prayer as a consciously focused activity—public or private, individual or corporate, formal or informal, in word or deed—in which people turn toward God in communion and conversation. In prayer we consciously focus on our relationship with God. We turn toward God because we need God.

There is wealth in this need. We need the God who is our Creator, our Lord. In prayer we thus recognize our finitude and we reach out to One whose life knows no beginning and no end. We need God, more intimately, as our Savior and Friend in time of need. That is why Christians, mindful of "trials and temptations," admonish one another to "take it to the Lord in prayer." We need Someone to care and to work at times when, and in situations where, our access, energy, and wisdom are dwarfed by the need. Our need for God is manifold.

May it be that we create what we need? If we speak of prayer and of

1

our need together, do we move toward those who would diagnose prayer as wish fulfillment? Does such needfelt prayer become, furthermore, a naysaying against the human, a denial of our worth and responsibility? It is possible, of course, that it does. The Christian cannot prove that it does not, for the knee bows in faith rather than argument. We do not cease to be human when we pray, and it is possible that our praying is *merely* human. And any human act is subject to corruption, including the corruption incurred in cursing the human in order to praise a God, real or imagined. But the Christian's claim is that to need God is not weakness but strength. And so it is that prayer becomes not impoverishment but empowerment. We pray because we need God. In prayer we meet the God we need—who may not much resemble the God we thought we needed, for God may have to surprise and judge in order to bless and save. In judgment and in salvation God is known as real in prayer. Again, there is wealth in this human need, as Søren Kierkegaard knew when he wrote that "man's need of God is his greatest perfection."[1]

We pray because we need God. But do we not already have God? Clearly, any God who could be either created or summoned by prayer would not be a God worth having. Indeed the one issuing the summons might rival such a God. But Christians pray because of God, who certainly wills and works without our prayers. Blaise Pascal understood this when he formulated God's word to the questing human: "Thou wouldst not seek Me, if thou didst not possess Me."[2] But the God who is already there before we pray is a God who seeks a personal relationship with us. Because of that divine will for relationship, we are called to move toward—not to create or to summon— God. In this living relationship there is to be life and growth. Prayer, which consciously focuses on the relationship, is particularly needed for such growth.

So we pray. And so we set about to study prayer. Our praying itself, as part of our living relationship with God, is to grow and mature. Of course this call to growth in prayer is not to be received as a counsel of perfection, an impossible ideal that effectively paralyzes us in our poor praying. The Christian is glad to repair with Paul, in Romans 8, to the Spirit who intercedes for us with sighs too deep for words. Yet the Christian does seek to "pray aright." Hence we study prayer. The Latin phrase *lex orandi, lex credendi* suggests that what we pray shapes what we believe. Often, in the history of the church, theologians in council assembled have affirmed what Christians in their liturgical practice and private devotions have already known. But we find that it works the other way as well. As we use our God-given minds we come more fully to understand our relationship with God, and our praying is changed.

In the present day there is particular need for the study of prayer. We live in a pluralistic society. Pluralism has long been a part of American experience. Our forebears came from many places and with divergent commitments. But the pace of pluralistic experience has intensified, and the scale has magnified. Pluralism does not in itself represent a threat. Rather it can contribute to a larger and richer whole. But there is a risk in this. Will commitment to pluralism lead us finally to indifference to commitment? Does pluralism mean tolerance, and tolerance the absence of conviction? If everybody's commitments are due equal respect, are they not all equally trivial?

The promise and peril of pluralism apply to our praying. We have a wealth of faith traditions. Few things are exotic any more. Indian gurus and Tibetan lamas are commonplace. Buddhists of many varieties flourish across the breadth of our land. There are strong Muslim communities, Sikh communities. And many of these people pray, or perhaps they meditate. Perhaps some things may be learned by us from them that will significantly enrich our praying. What is more, quite apart from recognized religious traditions, there is a renewed interest in spirituality in our society. A good argument can be made that prayer is "in." Prayer can no longer be dismissed as leftover baggage of the prescientific era or relegated to the periphery, for it has become a serious and passionate pursuit of many sophisticated moderns who are coming to view spirituality as a substantial and exciting discipline central to human experience. Thus new frontiers, insights, and alliances for exploring prayer are available. Within the church many are rediscovering traditions and disciplines long neglected for the renewing and nurturing of spirituality. Roman Catholic retreat houses are filled with Protestants. Surely it is a promising time.

But for the practice of prayer this pluralistic time may also be the worst of times. There are widespread practices that distort and betray Christian prayer. The One who graciously initiates communication through prayer must be scandalized by the human actions God is asked to bless in private, as well as in public, life. Our society abounds with self-righteous, sectarian, and even jingoistic prayers: "The Lord told me"; "Help our team trounce Central High"; "Believe and your farm mortgage will disappear"; "Lord, take away the threat of communism"; "Pray and you too can be rich." Wealth is blatantly condoned, and God's will is twisted, manipulated, and domesticated.

A related problem lies in the individualism spreading through American life. The belief that human beings are at bottom maximizers of self-interest and that social commitments and all cultural symbols are instrumental to the ends of individuals—a view propagated by some social scientists, particularly by psychologists and sociologists—steadily gains adherents. Daniel Bell has described this failure of commitment as

> the loss of *civitas*, that spontaneous willingness to obey the law, to respect the rights of others, to forgo the temptations of private enrichment at the expense of the public weal—in short, to honor the "city" of which one is a member. Instead, each man goes his own way, pursuing his private vices, which can be indulged only at the expense of public benefits.[3]

According to Robert Bellah,[4] most middle-class Americans today are engaged in the obsessive search for the "true self" cut loose from all communities of memory.

Obviously our praying is not immune to this individualistic virus. Christian faith recognizes the intimate personal character of the relationship with God, but it resists the privatization of faith by emphasizing the community of believers. The universal priesthood of believers links Christians with one another in responsibility and care; it does not isolate them in individual pipelines to God. Christians are called to the prayer of the church, and in this community they will come to gain the true selfhood intended by a God who created humankind in relationship ("Male and female created God them").

What is to prevent a pluralism without criteria from converging with an incipient individualism in a riotous disaster for the Christian church? The strategy of this book holds that question in mind. We do not start from scratch as we study prayer, for we have a heritage to guide us. The "norming norm" for the Christian is, of course, Scripture. Frederick Gaiser not only lifts up that standard for us but does so precisely with attention to the mutual critique and enrichment of corporate and individual prayer. With an eye on our own praying, Arland Hultgren examines the theme of expectations for prayer in the New Testament. The world of the New Testament turns out to be not so very different from our own, close enough to guide and judge us in any case. Building on that biblical material, Carl Volz directs our attention to the place of praise and discipline in the early church's understanding of prayer.

With that heritage, how are we to understand prayer in our own time? In the second section of the book, four efforts are made to respond to that question. The central category proves to be that of relationship. Terence Fretheim makes clear that this is not merely a contemporary fashion. Working closely with the biblical material, he shows that God has shared power with us and is thus open to being affected by us, for good or ill. In prayer, then, we use the gift of power in order to create more space in which God can work in the world. My own chapter follows this line of thought closely. It maintains that even the self-limitation of God demonstrates rather than diminishes the transcendence of God, for God is not less God in God's commitment to us. Accordingly, our prayers affect God and God's action in the world, as well as ourselves.

Paul Martinson develops the theme of relationship further in two respects. According to him, God must be understood (a) as a community, a Trinity, and (b) as seeking a relationship with "all that breathes." This is not a blanket endorsement of pluralism. Martinson is not arguing that all faiths are equal. The triune God is one; we are not, and our prayers will differ. But it may be that in the recognition of human otherness we can catch a glimpse of the holy Other who calls all to praise. Not only is the Christian called toward God but that call also sends us out into the world. Thus Loren Halvorson develops the connection between prayer and action. He notes that in our relationship with God we know both the control and the freedom we need. We come as deepened selves.to what we find to be a widened world.

Will we arrive there? Our study of prayer, rooted in the heritage and guided by Christian reflection, needs to arrive at faithful practice in our own lives. How are we, then, to pray? David Tiede begins the third section of the book with this clear biblical word: We are to pray as our Lord taught us. Our Lord invites the disciples, and he invites us, to join an immense human community called to the distinctive reign of justice and mercy. The words of the "kingdom prayer" can be found elsewhere, but for the Gospel writers Jesus' praying the prayer cannot be separated from the Easter reality of God's dominion on earth. So does Scripture instruct us. But the prayers of Christians have not always illustrated and served God's commitment to justice and mercy. Paul Sonnack shows that sad fact in his study of prayer in public life. He suggests that it may be precisely because prayer has been understood as private and individualistic in character that our presidents draw back from what they take to be a violation of both the public character of their office and the private character of their religion. And when we do pray in public, as in the halls of Congress, the prayers are often individualistic instruments for American advancement. Yet within Sonnack's analysis there sounds the possibility of true prayers for the common good, as in the prayers of Abraham Lincoln or occasionally in a prayer in Congress.

Christian prayer can be corrupted, both inside and outside the Christian community—that is clear. Hence we are called to learn and teach prayer rightly. Eugene Kreider picks up that theme and gives attention both to informal "modeling" in the community of prayer and to developing cognitive and affective understandings of prayer. Given the emphasis on the reality of the human in relationship with God, it follows that biological and social development and the quality and variety of the environment will make a difference in our learning to pray.

That prayer and the study of prayer are needed seems clear, no less clear in our time of pluralism and individualism. Believing that, we here offer our ten contributions.

NOTES

1. This is the title of one of Søren Kierkegaard's discourses from 1844. See his *Edifying Discourses*, vol. 4 (Minneapolis: Augsburg Pub. House, 1946).

2. Blaise Pascal, *Pensées* (New York: E. P. Dutton, 1958), 554.

3. Daniel Bell, *The Cultural Contradictions of Capitalism* (New York: Basic Books, 1976), 245.

4. See Robert N. Bellah, Richard Madsen, William M. Sullivan, Ann Swidler, and Steven M. Tipton, *Habits of the Heart: Individualism and Commitment in American Life* (Berkeley and Los Angeles: Univ. of California Press, 1985).

PART ONE

THE HERITAGE
OF PRAYER

One

INDIVIDUAL AND CORPORATE PRAYER IN OLD TESTAMENT PERSPECTIVE
Frederick J. Gaiser

FORMS OF PRAYER

Biblical studies sometimes employ methodologies with names that sound vaguely threatening. One of these is "form criticism"—the attempt to analyze and relate biblical texts according to certain typical literary forms. Actually, anyone who has ever recognized that some of the psalms are "I" prayers while others are "we" prayers has begun to engage in form criticism. If one couples the distinction between "I" and "we" prayers with another—that between psalms crying "out of the depths" and psalms that "shout for joy"—one arrives at four possible psalm forms (see figure).

Individual   Community

Lament   Praise

This simple exercise tells us something important about biblical prayer: that it is not all the same. It is obvious of course that different prayers have different contents, but form criticism points to different categories of prayers—prayers of different types, arising out of differing situations. This comes as no great surprise, since it reflects our own experience with prayer.

Consider two prayers that have many similarities in content and concern, yet display something quite different with respect to style and literary form:

> Lord, I'm hurting today, and I just want to ask you to send your Spirit to fill my heart and heal my body. I need you, Lord, and I know you have promised to help those who love you. Thank you, Lord, for sending Jesus as my Savior. I pray to you in his name and ask you to be with me so I can make it through the day. (Prayer of a seminarian)

> Almighty God, you have given us grace at this time with one accord to make our common supplication to you, and you have promised through your well-beloved Son that when two or three are gathered together in his name, you will be in the midst of them. Fulfill now, O Lord, our desires and petitions as may be best for us, granting us, in this world, knowledge of your truth and, in the age to come, life everlasting. (LBW prayer 212)

It may even be, though it is certainly not necessary, that those who pray either of these two prayers view the devotional life of those who pray the other with some suspicion. Many people pray fervently in highly personal terms but find the structured and confessionally cautious prayers of corporate liturgy sterile and meaningless. Others, perhaps uneasy in private devotion and uncomfortable with intensely personal prayer language, find solace and support, even warmth and piety, in the prayers of a communal liturgy.

There are similar distinctions in the Psalter. Laments there may be characterized by either the personal passionate intensity of Psalm 6 or the communal historical reflection of Psalm 80:

> Be gracious to me, O Lord, for I am languishing;
>   O Lord, heal me, for my bones are troubled. . . .
> I am weary with my moaning;
>   every night I flood my bed with tears;
>   I drench my couch with my weeping.
>   (Ps. 6:2, 6)

> Give ear, O Shepherd of Israel,
>   thou who leadest Joseph like a flock! . . .

> Thou didst bring a vine out of Egypt;
>   thou didst drive out the nations and plant it. . . .
> Turn again, O God of hosts!
>   Look down from heaven, and see;
> have regard for this vine,
>   the stock which thy right hand planted.
>   (Ps. 80:1, 8, 14–15)

A comparison of the individual and communal psalms of lament in the Old Testament may help us reflect on our own practice of prayer. Although our practice is obviously affected by more than the piety and worship of the psalmists, their writings, which the church has accepted into its canon, can provide at least a valuable case study for our consideration.

CORPORATE PUBLIC PRAYER

The corporate prayer of the Psalter is truly public in nature—that is, it has to do with the community as a whole in matters of genuinely common concern. It reflects the shared historical and political realities of the people of Israel. This is true not only in what it *asks* of God, that God should deliver the group from natural disaster or political catastrophe, but also in what it *assumes* of God, that God is both cosmic Creator and Lord of history. The two assumptions about God come together in Psalm 74, where Israel appeals to God's work both in creation and in Israel's corporate past:

> Thine is the day, thine also the night;
>   thou hast established the luminaries and the sun.
> Thou hast fixed all the bounds of the earth;
>   thou hast made summer and winter.
>   (Ps. 74:16–17)

> Remember thy congregation, which thou hast gotten of old,
>   which thou hast redeemed to be the tribe of thy heritage!
> Remember Mount Zion, where thou hast dwelt.
>   (Ps. 74:2)

In this prayer, the calamity is assumed to be the result of divine wrath:

> O God, why dost thou cast us off for ever?
>   Why does thy anger smoke against the sheep of thy pasture?
>   (Ps. 74:1)

Yet, the cries of why suggest that there is not merely a doctrine of tidy
retribution at work here:

> How long, O God, is the foe to scoff?
>> Is the enemy to revile thy name for ever?
> Why dost thou hold back thy hand,
>> why dost thou keep thy right hand in thy bosom?
>> (Ps. 74:10–11)

Although normally God's wrath is seen as the consequence of Israel's
sin (cf. Psalm 90:7–8), there is not always a clear sense of cause and effect relating crime and punishment:

> All this has come upon us,
>> though we have not forgotten thee,
>> or been false to thy covenant.
> Our heart has not turned back,
>> nor have our steps departed from thy way,
> that thou shouldst have broken us in the place of jackals,
>> and covered us with deep darkness.
>> (Ps. 44:17–19)

The enemy might be an active, and to some extent independent agent
in the reality of disaster:

> O God, do not keep silence;
>> do not hold thy peace or be still, O God!
> For lo, thy enemies are in tumult;
>> those who hate thee have raised their heads.
> They lay crafty plans against thy people;
>> they consult together against thy protected ones.
> They say, "Come, let us wipe them out as a nation;
>> let the name of Israel be remembered no more!"
>> (Ps. 83:1–4)

In summary, the community laments (of which the preceding
prayers are examples) confess that God, the Creator of the universe,
has become actively involved in a particular human history (that of Israel). God is so personally related to Israel that human pleas are clearly
understood to have their effect upon the divine. The desired result is
God's renewed intervention in history to bring wholeness and salvation to God's people. At the same time, the prayers recognize that there
are elements working against a simple outcome, elements that produce
a separation between God and his people. These include Israel's sin-

fulness, the chaotic work of others (Israel's enemies), and the finitude of creation itself (i.e., the why without clear answer, reflecting the realization that there is not always a simple solution to the problem of God's apparent absence).

These prayers frequently arrive at the very edge of the precipice of confusion and unbelief:

> Rouse thyself! Why sleepest thou, O Lord?
> Awake! Do not cast us off for ever!
> Why dost thou hide thy face?
> Why dost thou forget our affliction and oppression?
> (Ps. 44:23–24)

Yet, their persistent credal remembrance of God's work in Israel's history and their ongoing attempts to state that belief in clear confessional statements keep them from falling into the abyss:

> We have heard with our ears, O God,
>   our fathers have told us,
> what deeds thou didst perform in their days,
>   in the days of old;
> thou with thy own hand didst drive out the nations,
>   but them thou didst set free;
> for not by their own sword did they win the land,
>   nor did their own arm give them victory;
> but thy right hand, and thy arm,
>   and the light of thy countenance;
> for thou didst delight in them.
> (Ps. 44:1–3)

This type of communal prayer is clearly attested in the Old Testament. The appropriate occasions are named by Solomon at the dedication of the temple (1 Kings 8:33–40). We can even experience something of the shape of the liturgy at the time of a postexilic locust plague:

> Blow the trumpet in Zion;
>   sanctify a fast;
> call a solemn assembly;
>   gather the people.
> Sanctify the congregation;
>   assemble the elders;
> gather the children,
>   even nursing infants.
> Let the bridegroom leave his room,

and the bride her chamber.
Between the vestibule and the altar
   let the priests, the ministers of the Lord, weep
and say, "Spare thy people, O Lord. . . ."
                                                    (Joel 2:15–17)

INDIVIDUAL PRIVATE PRAYER

The discussion of the place of individual prayer in the Old Testament is somewhat trickier. There is not the same kind of agreement about the role of private piety in Israel that there is about the role of public piety. It is easy to see that there are psalms in which prayer is offered by an "I," but what does that mean? Part of the problem is exhibited by the Song of the Sea (Exodus 15:1–18). Although this is formally an "I" prayer, it is clear that Moses speaks here for all Israel. Might that not be true for all the "individual" psalms? Should we always read the "I" as a collective or royal "I," meaning to speak of and for the whole people? Many would claim this, arguing that "private" piety arises only at a stage of human development later than that of the primitive, tribal society of ancient Israel, where "it is often hard to distinguish between individual and collective prayers, or between private and liturgical prayers."[1]

Yet, there do seem to be genuinely individual prayers. The laments of the prophet Jeremiah, growing out of the awful torment of being called to preach judgment to his beloved people, are so like the "I" laments of the Psalter that there is no reason to assume that the latter cannot also be truly individual:

Righteous art thou, O Lord, when I complain to thee;
   yet I would plead my case before thee.
Why does the way of the wicked prosper?
Why do all who are treacherous thrive?
                                                    (Jer. 12:1–3)

Hannah's infertility reflects a situation tragically familiar to some women in every age. By borrowing language from the individual lament psalms to tell her story, the biblical narrator (1 Samuel 1) shows us that prayers of the Psalter can indeed fit the need and piety of individual Israelites. Consider Psalm 10: changing the gender of the pronouns and the final word from "fatherless" to "childless" would make this prayer beautifully suitable for Hannah's need. Each of the starred words is used (in the Hebrew text) in just the same way in her story:[2]

> The hapless is crushed, sinks down,
>   and falls by his might.
> He thinks in his heart, "God has forgotten*,
>   he has hidden his face, he will never see* it."
> Arise, O Lord; O God, lift up thy hand;
>   forget* not the afflicted*. . . .
> Thou didst see*; yea, thou dost note trouble and vexation*,
>   that thou mayest take it into thy hands;
> the hapless commits himself to thee;
>   thou hast been the keeper of the fatherless.
>   (Ps. 10:10–12, 14)

What is the nature of this individual prayer piety in ancient Israel? Despite many similarities, there are significant differences between the individual lament psalms and the communal lament psalms— differences reflecting a personal family piety that was perhaps quite distinct from the official public piety of Israel.[3]

Whereas in the community laments, the appeal to God is made on the basis of God's datable historical acts in behalf of Israel, the corresponding confession of trust in the individual laments refers to a personal relationship between the "I" and God which has accompanied the "I" through life since birth. Yahweh is addressed intimately as "my God." There is normally no mention of saving history in the individual laments; the divine-human relationship is based on God's creation of the individual:

> For thou, O Lord, art my hope,
>   my trust, O Lord, from my youth.
> Upon thee I have leaned from my birth;
>   thou art he who took me from my mother's womb.
> My praise is continually of thee.
>   (Ps. 71:5–6)

The enemies in the community laments are political and military foes whose attacks (now past) have decimated Israel. The enemies in the individual laments, once perhaps demonic powers, are now the mocking neighbors and friends who threaten the existence of the one praying:

> My enemies say of me in malice:
> "When will he die, and his name perish?"

And when one comes to see me, he utters empty words,
while his heart gathers mischief;
when he goes out, he tells it abroad. . . .
Even my bosom friend in whom I trusted,
who ate of my bread, has lifted his heel against me.
(Ps. 41:5–9)

These differences suggest that there was in Israel a distinction between individual or family piety and the official national cult. The one was founded in individual creation, based on an ongoing personal relationship with God, and was concerned with personal healing and security over against the powers of death invading present existence. The other was founded in Yahweh's historical acts for Israel, based on his promises to save, and was concerned with the ongoing security of the whole people and the proper definition of its God over against the gods of the nations. The community lament and its religious expression were located in the Jerusalem temple and practiced by the gathered congregation of Israel. The individual lament and its piety may, in contrast, have been at home within the family or tribal unit in its local worship.

Might, then, the real differences between individual and corporate prayer extend all the way back to biblical times? Are the two kinds of prayer inherent in human religious experience? Is the gap between individual and corporate piety unbridgeable? Are we doomed to an ongoing alienation between the adherents of the two?

INDIVIDUAL AND COMMUNAL PRAYER:
TWO PHENOMENA, ONE FAITH

We must be careful not to make too much of the distinction between individual and communal piety in ancient Israel—as real as that distinction is. A neat separation is not finally possible for a variety of reasons.

1. The present canonical shape of the Psalter is a powerful witness to the fact that in the end Israel did not regard the two pieties as mutually exclusive. Someone has put them together, mixed with virtual abandon, in a single book. Individual prayers have been given superscripts that relate them to congregational worship.[4] At the same time, com-

munal songs by being collected and written down have been made available for personal meditation (cf. Ps. 1:2).[5]

Even if all this editing and collecting is a late activity, the stereotypical language of even the earliest laments suggests communal influence on individual or familial piety. Although the awful lament questions (Why? How long?) betray spontaneous emotion, the language and structure of the lament psalms are clearly shaped by convention. These prayers have been reworked by "professional" hands. They are held in trust by the community to be made available to the individual when the need arises. In great distress, few are able to be great poets or prayer writers. "I am so troubled that I cannot speak" (Ps. 77:4b). But the community has collected prayers for occasions of affliction and by making them available provides the one praying with a language that could not have been achieved without help. This language provides a way of response that by bringing turmoil into contact with God breaks out of chaos and moves toward healing.

2. An important part of the distress of the individual laments is isolation:

> Thou hast caused my companions to shun me;
>   thou hast made me a thing of horror to them.
> I am shut in so that I cannot escape.
>
> (Ps. 88:8)

The one praying knows, with God, that "it is not good that the human should be alone" (Gen. 2:18). But the problem is precisely that the other, who was meant by God to be helper and support, has become enemy:

> My companion stretched out his hand against his friends,
>   he violated his covenant.
> His speech was smoother than butter,
>   yet war was in his heart;
> his words were softer than oil,
>   yet they were drawn swords.
>
> (Ps. 55:20–21)

The intention of these prayers is that the isolation be overcome. The alienated sufferer asks God for reentry into the credal worship of the congregation:

> I will tell of thy name to my brethren;
> in the midst of the congregation I will praise thee.
> (Ps. 22:22)

The goal of the individual prayers of lamentation is not a renewed "private" religion, it is restoration to the full worshiping community.

3. Of no small importance to these psalms is the address. Especially since there is considerable commonality between Israel's laments and those of other cultures, the source of help to which the prayer is addressed is particularly significant. In Israel, both individual and communal laments are addressed to Yahweh. The name Yahweh, introduced in the exodus (Exod. 3:14–15; 6:2–3) and associated with the covenant (Exod. 20:2), immediately draws the individual's prayer into the framework of God's historical and political activity for the entire community.

4. The individual psalms of narrative praise are proclamations of deliverance made by some whose laments have been answered. A constant feature of these prayers is the essential relationship between individual and community. The one praying describes what God has done for him or her, and then calls upon the faithful in the congregation to join in praise:

> O Lord, thou hast brought up my soul from Sheol,
> restored me to life from among those gone down to the Pit.
> Sing praises to the Lord, O you his saints,
> and give thanks to his holy name.
> (Ps. 30:3–4)

It is clear from this that the community needs the individual. The deliverance of the one becomes the deliverance of all.

As we have seen, in the community lament Israel complains that God is not currently active. At one level, the individual's narrative praise gives answer to that lament, which is shown by the community's willingness to associate the saving act for the individual with the saving acts for Israel:

> Come and see what God has done:
> he is terrible in his deeds among men.
> He turned the sea into dry land;
> men passed through the river on foot. . . .

> Come and hear, all you who fear God,
> and I will tell what he has done for me.
> (Ps. 66:5–6, 16)

On the other hand, the individual needs the community. As is always the case in the Bible, the description of God's saving act extends to and embraces the response of praise to the saving act. For the individual Israelite, both liturgical rubrics and apparent inner compulsion required offering this praise before the community. The experience of deliverance was not complete until this was accomplished.

How is the individual to know that a "religious" experience is not just the result of "an undigested bit of beef, a blot of mustard, a crumb of cheese, a fragment of an underdone potato" (to which Scrooge wanted to attribute his vision of Marley's ghost)? By offering a report to the community for use in its praise, the individual seeks acceptance of the experience. Only if there was a true intervention of God is the report worthy to be taken up in the community's praise.

FORMING PRAYERS

The Old Testament will not finally allow us to choose one or the other of the pieties described in this chapter. It describes both, refining and sharpening each in its relation to the other. To the degree that Israel's experience can inform our own, several observations seem possible. Chief among these is an extrapolation into the present of the kind of check-and-balance principle we observed in the Old Testament relationship between communal and individual piety.

There is always something wild and uncontained about individual personal testimony to God's work in the world—which perhaps inevitably makes it suspect in the view of a church whose corporate and public responsibility includes defining and identifying as clearly as possible the manner and place of God's work in our behalf. On the other hand, the public worship shaped by such definition is always subject to the sins of dogmatic formalism and bureaucratic control. When this happened in the Old Testament era, those true individuals the prophets rose up in rebellion:

> I hate, I despise your feasts,
> and I take no delight in your solemn assemblies. . . .

Take away from me the noise of your songs;
to the melody of your harps I will not listen.
But let justice roll down like waters,
and righteousness like an ever-flowing stream.
(Amos 5:21, 23–24)

Those songs that Amos despised were not alien melodies, they were the psalms. But now prayed hypocritically, they had become enemies to true faith.[6]

The true voice of individual piety serves the people of God in a prophetic manner, challenging and maybe even praying against a corporate expression of the faith that has become too closely associated with the celebration of the status quo. Yet it must be admitted that individual laments too can support a tamed and mechanical understanding of religion and God. What happens if the response to an individual petition becomes routine and expected? Then a living encounter with God becomes a mere salvation automat—for every lament a quick word of divine assurance and an all too easy jump to praise:

To be sure, in the days of the prayer meeting a man or a woman sometimes came to the meeting with a genuine experience to share. But often such persons, like most of the rest of us, talked too soon. That is, the experience had not been given time to ripen, to become part of a life pattern. Whatever of spiritual energy was being generated, leaked out too readily in words.[7]

What saved Israel from a too easy assurance was the recognition that God's response to the lament belongs alone to God. It may be long in coming (Jer. 17:15). It may not be heard at all (Psalm 88). Instead of promising immediate healing, it may instead call upon the one praying to wait—to live in faith and hope rather than in sight and glory:

Wait for the Lord;
be strong, and let your heart take courage;
yea, wait for the Lord!
(Ps. 27:14; cf. Ps. 130:5–7)

God might challenge the very premise of the lament:

Why do you say, O Jacob,
and speak, O Israel,
"My way is hid from the Lord,
and my right is disregarded by my God"?

> Have you not known? Have you not heard?
> The Lord is the everlasting God,
>   the Creator of the ends of the earth.
> He does not faint or grow weary,
>   his understanding is unsearchable.
>   (Isa. 40:27–28)

Terrifyingly, God might even say no (Jer. 14:10). For a study of prayer there is perhaps no more sobering biblical reference than this one:

> Thou hast wrapped thyself with anger and pursued us,
>   slaying without pity;
> thou hast wrapped thyself with a cloud
>   so that no prayer can pass through.
>   (Lam. 3:43–44)

To be sure, God's hesitation or challenge or rebuke never compromised God's committed compassion for Israel. The invitation to return was always present (Isa. 55:6–7), for Israel had learned to pray with confidence and expectation not because of who Israel was but because of who God was. Yet because God's answer was open (a personal response to each occasion in its distinctiveness), not every psalm met a ready divine response. Israel lived in the same world we do, a world where divine intervention, though confidently hoped for, is our delightful surprise, not our expected due.

Today, just as in the days of the Old Testament, the prayers of the faithful will find both individual and corporate expression. In the biblical record, the individual lament and the personal experience of answered prayer produced audacious and prophetic witness to the living work of God. Christians would do well to find ways to speak and to hear this voice in their devotional life. At the same time, God's healing or rescue of individuals was not in itself the heart of Israel's prayer or proclamation. That healing was a sign of God's saving action for all and needed to be tested by the communal and confessional understanding of God's work.[8] It is this understanding that lies behind the strong community laments and thanksgivings of the Psalter.

The mutual critique and enrichment of public and private, of corporate and individual, piety was an integral aspect of Old Testament theology. It will continue to be integral to a healthy church. Neither individual prayer nor corporate prayer has a claim to exclusivity or to superiority as an expression of Christian piety. Each has its place in the biblical tradition.

NOTES

1. Roland de Vaux, *Ancient Israel: Its Life and Institutions* (New York: McGraw-Hill, 1965), 2:458.

2. Frederick J. Gaiser, "Songs in the Story" (diss., Univ. of Heidelberg, 1984), 207.

3. Rainer Albertz, *Persönliche Frömmigkeit und offizielle Religion: Religionsinterner Pluralismus in Israel und Babylon* (Stuttgart: Calwer Verlag, 1978). The differences between Old Testament individual and community laments presented here are based on Albertz's work.

4. E.g., the intensely personal experience of Psalm 30 was eventually used for the community's Hanukkah celebration, a celebration observing the Maccabean victory over the Greeks.

5. Similar observations can be made with regard to particular psalms. A final verse is added to Psalm 25, allowing the individual prayer to speak for all Israel. Psalm 51 moves from personal repentance to anticipation of renewed sacrifices in a rebuilt temple. Psalm 102 simply jumps back and forth between individual lament and communal/credal affirmation.

6. Another example is found in Isaiah 51, where the prophet apparently responds directly to Psalm 44. At one time that psalm had wrestled with the awful reality that destruction had come upon Israel "though we have not forgotten thee" (v. 17). Later, however, these words had become hollow and needed to be combated by the prophet: "Who are you that you . . . have forgotten the Lord, your Maker?" (Isa. 51:12–13).

7. Margueritte Harmon Bro, *More Than We Are* (New York: Harper & Row, 1965 [1948], 105.

8. A fine example is the song of Hannah (1 Samuel 2), which makes God's deliverance of her ("My strength [horn] is exalted in the Lord," v. 1) into a sign of God's saving activity for Israel through David ("He will exalt the power [horn] of his anointed," v. 10).

Two

EXPECTATIONS OF PRAYER IN THE NEW TESTAMENT
Arland J. Hultgren

In a book on worship in early Christianity, Ferdinand Hahn has made the remark that for Jesus "prayer cannot be anything other than an expression of confidence,"[1] a confidence grounded in a certainty of the nearness of God and God's readiness to hear.

The expression of confidence of which Hahn writes is not new or unique to Jesus, for it is found already, for example, in the Psalms of ancient Israel. The Psalmist cries out, "Answer me, O Lord my God," and declares, "I have trusted in your steadfast love" (13:3, 5). But what is particularly striking in the case of Jesus is that he not only demonstrates an astonishing confidence in his own prayers but he commends it to others in his teaching:

> Ask, and it will be given to you; seek, and you will find; knock, and it will be opened to you. . . . What man of you, if his son asks him for bread, will give him a stone? Or if he asks for a fish, will give him a serpent? If you then, who are evil, know how to give good gifts to your children, how much more will your Father who is in Heaven give good things to those who ask him!" (Matt. 7:7–11)

Moreover, an expression of confidence in prayer appears not only in the teachings and practice of Jesus presented in the Gospels. It appears again and again throughout the New Testament.

23

The New Testament contains a rich display of instances of prayer, admonitions to pray, and instructions on prayer. It is not our purpose to provide even a brief survey of these. Our aim is more modest: to ask the question, What are the expectations of prayer in the New Testament? What kind and degree of confidence are expressed? The question has been formulated out of both a theological and a pastoral concern. Whenever we reflect on the practice of prayer, we are justified in asking why we or anyone else should pray. What comes out of it? What are our expectations? All kinds of claims are made about prayer and what it will do—about what one can expect from it. Such claims are based on experience (our own, or that of others as reported to us), data from the Scriptures, data from the history of the church, and theological considerations. For example, one person might quote the saying of Jesus in Matthew 21:22: "Whatever you ask in prayer, you will receive, if you have faith." The implication is that if a person truly believes, his or her prayers will be answered. But another person might object that quoting this verse can be misleading, for there are instances in the New Testament itself, as well as in common experience, when requests made of God are not fulfilled.

Since there are competing claims about prayer, it can be instructive to investigate what New Testament faith expected of prayer. Our own expectations should have a family resemblance to those found in the writings of the New Testament. To guide us in our times, we are justified in asking what early Christians expected of prayer in theirs. Our discussion will be ordered around three kinds of expectations, which also turn out to be related to three kinds of prayer: (*a*) expectations concerning God, as seen in invocations; (*b*) expectations concerning others, as seen in intercessions; and (*c*) expectations concerning oneself and one's community as seen in petitions.

EXPECTATIONS CONCERNING
GOD: INVOCATIONS

Under the first category we include prayers that have to do essentially with God—with God's rule and glory. In the Old Testament there are prayers for God to establish his glory throughout the universe (Pss. 72:19; 102:12–17; 108:5), and in the ancient prayer known as the kaddish the Jew prayed that God would establish his kingdom.[2]

Such prayers presuppose that at the present moment the rule and glory of God are not universally acknowledged and that, consequently, people do not serve God as they ought. Prayers are made for God to establish his glory and rule throughout the world so that all people might serve him aright, with the result that there might be universal peace, justice, and well-being. It goes without saying that in this kind of prayer there are positive ends in view for humanity, but through such prayers people ask of and expect from God a measure of activity by which God's power, if not God himself, is revealed to the glory of God, so that humanity will respond by right worship and service.

This kind of prayer is so commonplace for modern Christians, because of its use in the Lord's Prayer ("Your kingdom come"), that it is virtually taken for granted as typical of prayer utterances. Yet it is a kind of prayer that has flourished particularly in the Judeo-Christian tradition. It is in the Judeo-Christian tradition that history is considered to have a linear direction toward a goal in which God will transform the whole creation into a "new heaven and a new earth" (Isa. 65:17; Rev. 21:1). In the present, at least in Christian thought, the creation is considered to exist in a fallen state. But prayers are offered by Christians for God to exercise his reign and his will on earth within history in the making, and fully at the coming of Christ in his glory, when all things will be subjected to God.

Prayers in the New Testament that invoke the advent of God have to do with each person of the Trinity. Concerning God the Father, the petition is made in the Lord's Prayer that God's name be hallowed, his kingdom come, and his will be done (Matt. 6:9–10; cf. Luke 11:2). Concerning the Son, there is the petition "Maranatha" (1 Cor. 16:21), which is an Aramaic utterance meaning "Our Lord, come" that is also found in Greek translation (Rev. 22:20) and then again as an Aramaic expression in the early second century (*Didache* 10.6). Concerning the Spirit, the promise is given in the Gospel of Luke that God will give the Holy Spirit to those who ask (11:13). And in the Gospel of John, Jesus prays to the Father to send the Spirit (or Paraclete, 14:16) to those who believe, and he expresses certainty that this will happen (14:26).

These prayers and teachings on prayer concerning the advent of God into the world are expressed with the highest of all expectations. Never are doubts expressed whether this sort of prayer will be answered. It is taken for granted that it is appropriate to make, and expect the fulfillment of, petitions that ask God to be God, to establish his kingdom, and to send his Spirit. And the maranatha prayer addressed to the risen Lord, beseeching him to come, is expressed in the most terse and fervent way; the one promised to return is entreated to come.

But regardless of the intensity of expectations, it is clear that there were some adjustments in the expectations held. Although the early church experienced the coming of the Spirit, it did not experience the coming of the kingdom of God in its fullness and the Parousia of Christ. Surely the church must have come to realize that these petitions were not being fulfilled. Surely the expectations expressed in these acts of invocation must have been tempered by the passing of time—at least in some quarters, if not in all.

Texts show that to be the case. There was a tempering of expectations but not an abandonment of them. The apostle Paul expressed in 1 Thessalonians, one of his earliest letters, the expectation that the coming of Christ would be soon; it would be within the lifetime of Paul and his contemporaries (4:15–17). And the Gospel of Mark assumes as a matter of course that the kingdom of God will come soon (1:15; 9:1; 15:43). The expectation of the imminence of both the Parousia of Christ and the kingdom of God, however, was relaxed with the passing of time. Paul himself seems to have come to realize, by the time he wrote one of his later letters, that the Parousia would not occur before his own death (Phil. 1:22–24), and in the Gospel of Luke—written later than Mark's Gospel—both the Parousia of Christ and the coming of the kingdom are considered to be farther into the future (19:11; 21:8–9; cf. 17:20–21; 22:69).

Yet even though the expectations of the advent of the kingdom and of the Christ appear to have been tempered with the passing of time (at least for some writers), the expectations were not abandoned. The Lord's Prayer, invoking the coming of the kingdom, was still prayed in the community of Matthew late in the first century, and in that of the *Didache* (8.2) early in the second. The maranatha prayer for the Parousia of Christ was prayed by John the Seer near the end of the first century (Rev. 22:20) and also in the community of the *Didache* (10.6) in the second century. It belongs to the very heart of the Christian tradition to pray for the coming of God's kingdom and for the advent of the Son of God in glory. To the present day the church prays for the coming of the kingdom of God by its use of the Lord's Prayer, and during the season of Advent its members join in those sturdy prayers which begin, "Stir up your power, O Lord, and come . . ."

For Christians of all times and places, the reality of God—as known through the story of Israel and the Christ—entails an understanding that God acts to manifest his glory and to save his people. In spite of all that would appear to prove the opposite, at the basis of all things is God, the living God, who wills the redemption of all that he has made and acts in history and at history's end to accomplish it. Resistance and rebellion are recognized, but the thought that God is unwilling or unable to bring history to its end and to restore creation to its intended quality and purpose is unthinkable.

The biblical imagery of the coming of the kingdom and the advent of the Christ may seem rather quaint to some, even many, readers of the New Testament today. Yet it is an imagery that can inspire hope and the betterment of life for all people. Prayers for the advent of God and his Christ can be interpreted as the cries of protest against prevailing conditions in the world; and they are that, but they are more than that. They are the cries of those who believe that reality is greater than the ambiguities of history and the expanse of the physical universe, that reality has a transcendent dimension as well, and that reality can be affected by the energies of prayer. Prayers for the kingdom of God and for the advent of the Christ rest on the view that the biblical story reveals the character of reality in its making toward a goal, that reality as seen and experienced is not final, and that all things will finally be transformed. The hope is expressed that this transformation will take place quickly. All of this is portrayed by means of vivid imagery in the Bible: the wolf shall dwell with the lamb (Isa. 11:6), the nations shall be miraculously healed by leaves coming forth from a tree of life that in turn is watered by a river flowing from the throne of God (Rev. 22:1–2). Christians pray without reservations for God to be God and to establish his rule and glory over all things, and it is expected that God will indeed do so.

EXPECTATIONS CONCERNING OTHERS: INTERCESSIONS

Prayers of intercession for others are found in the Old Testament. They are offered by the patriarchs and Moses (Gen. 18:22–32; Exod.

5:22–23; 32:11–13), by David (2 Sam. 12:16–18), and by various prophets (Amos 7:1–6; Ezek. 9:8; 11:13). These intercessions are usually for the people in general. But there are also intercessions for individuals (1 Kings 17:20; 2 Kings 4:32–33), including gentile rulers and their domains (Jer. 29:7; Ezra 6:10). Josephus (1st cent. A.D.) regarded intercessions as more important than petitions for one's own needs: "Prayers for the welfare of the community must take precedence of those for ourselves; for we are born for fellowship, and he who sets [the community's] claims above his private interests is specially acceptable to God" (*Against Apion* 2.196).[3]

Within the New Testament, intercessions for others have several kinds of objects, six of them particularly prominent. First, there are intercessions for the growth of others in spiritual maturity (Eph. 1:16–17; Phil. 1:9; Col. 1:9). Second, there are those asking that the gospel or the Christian witness may be extended through the ministry of others (Eph. 6:18–20; Col. 4:3; 2 Thess. 3:1). Third, there are petitions and exhortations to pray for the physical healing of others (Acts 9:40; 28:8; James 5:13–16). Fourth, there are prayers for the deliverance of others from perilous conditions, such as imprisonment, and for safety in travel (Acts 12:5–12; Rom. 15:30–32; Phil. 1:19; Heb. 13:18–19). Fifth, there are prayers for ruling authorities and for civil order (1 Tim. 2:1–2). And finally, there are prayers made, or to be made, for persons outside, or even opposed to, the Christian movement: Jesus instructs his followers to pray for their persecutors (Matt. 5:44/Luke 6:28) "so that," he says, "you may be sons of your Father who is in heaven; for he makes his sun rise on the evil and the good, and sends rain on the just and on the unjust" (Matt. 5:45); and Paul prays that unbelieving Israel might be saved (Rom. 10:1).

As in the case with prayers for the coming of God's kingdom and the advent of Christ, intercessions for others in the New Testament are made or prescribed with high expectations. As one reads through the prayers of the New Testament and its teaching on prayer, one is struck by the awesome trust displayed regarding the presumed efficacy of intercessions for others. For example, there are the words of the Letter to James: "Is any among you sick? Let him call for the elders of the church, and let them pray over him, anointing him with oil in the name of the Lord; and the prayer of faith will save the sick man, and the Lord will raise him up" (5:14–15).

Yet it is evident that intercessions for others could not be, and were not, always fulfilled exactly in the ways expected. When Paul prayed for the salvation of unbelieving Israel, he most certainly had their conversion in mind, but that did not happen. Later in the same letter he concluded that Israel's salvation would be by the mercy of God rather than through faith in the gospel (Rom. 11:25–32). In spite of Paul's request for prayers at Rome for his safety in Jerusalem and for a safe arrival at Rome (Rom. 15:30–32), he was arrested at Jerusalem and was taken to Rome in custody (Acts 21—28). And in spite of the illustrations of healing through intercessory prayer in Acts, and in spite of exhortations for intercessions for the sick in James, prayers for healing surely did not avail in all cases. Can we assume that there were no prayers of intercession for those in Corinth who became sick and died (1 Cor. 11:30)? Not all Christians of the apostolic age died of martyrdom! They lived at a time when the life expectancy was about twenty-five years for newborn females and twenty-three years for males, when only one newborn in eight could be expected to reach forty, and when people were virtually defenseless against typhoid, malaria, tuberculosis, pneumonia, and many other ailments.[4] Christians cannot be excluded from these statistics. In fact, the healings of the sick through prayer in Acts were taken to be extraordinary acts of the apostolic era; that is why they were recorded. And the exhortation in James is ambiguous in what it promises: it may be that the Lord will save the sick person and raise that person to health on earth, but if not, the Lord will surely save the sick person and raise him or her to life in the world to come.

To raise questions about the efficacy of intercessions is thus not simply a matter of "modern rationalism" at work. There are bits and pieces of evidence within the New Testament itself that show that the writers were not as confident as we might think. There is some element of reserve even in the midst of expectations.

A question for the Christian of today is whether there can be any "reentry" into the world of expectation which the Bible portrays in its illustrations of, and prescriptions for, intercession. If there can be no expectations, what is the use of interceding? Yet for many thoughtful Christians there are few aspects of worship more important to the individual Christian and the congregation than intercession. The congregation that prays fervently for peace, justice, the healing of the sick

and troubled, the feeding of the poor, the liberation of the downtrod-
den, and for the extension of the gospel in the world is engaged in an
activity that is central to its identity and mission. A congregation that
dispenses with intercessions is abandoning the historic, apostolic, and
catholic view of the mission of God in the world. As we have seen,
prayers for others are common in the New Testament, and they are
prayed with expectation. The question is not raised whether verifiable
results will be seen. Immediate results are not the issue. The issue is
whether those who claim to belong to Christ will enlarge their vision
and circle of concerns to include all who are in need. Prayer must be
uttered in fervent expectation, not in a spirit of resignation to present
circumstances, for it is the expectation of Christians that history in the
making is guided by transcendent forces pervading all of reality, both
human and beyond.

EXPECTATIONS CONCERNING ONESELF AND
ONE'S COMMUNITY: PETITIONS

The most common form of prayer in the religions of the world is undoubtedly petition, in which one asks God or the gods for some good
for oneself or one's community. Prayer is defined in that way, for example, in a passage from Plato: "Prayer is a request made to a god," and
therefore one should "be scrupulously careful not inadvertently to ask
for a curse in mistake for a blessing" (*Laws* 7.80a–b).[5] The discussion
has to do with the care that must be taken in the composition of
prayers by poets. Their duty is to write prayers that call upon the gods
to bless the city.

Petitions are offered up in the Old Testament for the necessities of
life (1 Kings 8:22–53; Prov. 30:8), deliverance from enemies (Gen.
32:11; Pss. 31:15; 59:1), and guidance in making decisions (Gen.
24:12–14; Num. 11:11–15). Above all, there is the majestic prayer of
Solomon, who asks for wisdom (1 Kings 3:5–14).

The New Testament continues the tradition of asking God for benefits for oneself and one's community. Best known are the "we" petitions of the Lord's Prayer (Matt. 6:11–13). These, along with other
passages in the New Testament, exhibit a wide range of things for
which early Christians ask, or for which they are exhorted to ask. First,
they are to ask for daily necessities (Matt. 6:11; 7:11; Phil. 4:6). One of

the striking things in Matthew's Gospel is the declaration that God knows all that a person needs before that person asks (6:7–8, 32) but that, even though it is not necessary to inform God about one's needs, a person should ask anyway (6:11; 7:7–11). Second, Christians ask for forgiveness of sins (Matt. 6:12; cf. Luke 18:13–14). Third, they are to ask to be spared from the final testing that is to come upon the world: "Lead us not to the test" (Matt. 6:13). Here it is assumed that without God's help even the most fervent follower of Jesus is likely to fall away. Fourth, there is the exhortation to ask for spiritual wisdom (James 1:5) and even for the Holy Spirit (Luke 11:9–13). And finally, those who endure physical suffering are invited to pray (James 5:13). Paul records that he prayed for release from a certain "thorn in the flesh" (2 Cor. 12:9), which was undoubtedly a chronic illness or physical handicap (cf. Gal. 4:13–14).

It is in the realm of petitions for the self and the community that expectations appear to range most widely in the New Testament. At one end of the spectrum there is the saying of Jesus in Matthew's Gospel: "Whatever you ask in prayer, you will receive, if you have faith" (21:22). The saying has parallels in other Gospels (cf. Mark 11:24; John 15:7, 16; 16:23–24), and its confidence is reflected in passages from two epistles of the New Testament: "You do not have, because you do not ask" (James 4:2); ". . . and we receive from [God] whatever we ask" (1 John 3:22).

But there is evidence in the New Testament that expectations were not always that high. The two epistles just cited temper their own statements. The author of James goes on to say, "You ask and do not receive, because you ask wrongly, to spend it on your passions" (4:3), and near the end of 1 John there is the saying "This is the confidence which we have in [the Son of God], that if we ask anything according to his will he hears us" (5:14). There is the presumption in both cases that petitions can be unworthy of the divine-human relationship. That for which one prays must be in keeping with the will of God. This does not mean that prayer effects no change in God or response from God that would not otherwise take place. Prayer can prompt God. For example, in the parable of the unjust judge (Luke 18:1–8) the judge vindicates an oppressed widow because she keeps coming to him with her petitions and nearly wears him out; Jesus adds, "Will not God vindicate his elect, who cry to him day and night?" (18:7). Luke says that Jesus told this parable to his hearers "to the effect that they ought always to pray and not lose heart" (18:1). But petitions that make requests contrary to the will of God cannot of course receive a positive response from God. There are also instances of failed prayer in the New Testament. Perhaps the best known is Paul's request in prayer for release from the "thorn in the flesh" that continued to bother him or, in his own words, "harassed" him "to keep [him] from being too elated" (2 Cor. 12:7): "Three times I besought the Lord about this, that it should leave me; but he said to me, 'My grace is sufficient for you, for my power is made perfect in weakness'" (12:8–9). One would expect that Paul, the greatest apostle of the New Testament era, would be physically strong, eloquent, and have his prayers answered according to his requests. But instead he is physically weak (2 Cor. 10:10; 11:29–30; 12:5; Gal. 4:13–14) and lacking in eloquence (1 Cor. 2:4; 2 Cor. 10:10; 11:6), and his prayers are not always answered as he wants them to be. Moreover, even Jesus asks for deliverance from his forthcoming crucifixion, according to the Gospel accounts, in Gethsemane: "Abba, Father, all things are possible to thee; remove this cup from me" (Mark 14:36; cf. Matt. 26:39; Luke 22:42). The request is, of course, toned down by Jesus' concession to what the will of the father is: ". . . yet not what I will, but what thou wilt" (Mark 14:36; cf. Matt. 26:39; Luke 22:42). Even Jesus, who prays for what he wishes, has to concede that God's will must take precedence over his own. Finally, it is worth noting that it is not simply a matter of requests for "outer" necessities or desires (physical needs, healing, etc.) which may be denied. Immediately after the Lord's Prayer in the Gospel of Matthew it is taught that, even though one ask for forgiveness of sins—which should surely be granted—God will actually not forgive the "trespasses" of those who refuse to forgive others (6:15). The same point is made in the parable of the unforgiving servant (Matt. 18:23–35) and in the Gospel of Mark (11:25). The actual intent of such passages is probably hortatory rather than doctrinal, for how can anyone actually forgive others as fully and freely as God? The intention is to move persons to forgive others: how can a person expect to be forgiven by God if that person does not forgive others? As God forgives, so should we (Eph. 4:32; Col. 3:13). Nevertheless, the point is made in connection with teachings about prayer. One should not expect God to grant everything for which one prays. One should not expect even "spiritual" blessings (such as forgiveness) when one's petition arises from a heart and mind opposed to the will of God.

A review of expectations regarding petitions for oneself and one's community shows that there is a wide range. There are statements in the New Testament that encourage petitions on the grounds that God gives fully and freely to the person who asks in faith. Yet thoughtful Christians of today approach such passages with a measure of reserve or even skepticism. Experience does not always bring what seems to be promised. And the response that all that is needed is greater faith does not remove the skepticism. It may simply induce anger.

There is, however, a measure of reserve if not skepticism within the New Testament itself, as well as illustrations of failed prayer and teachings to the effect that God does not grant even "spiritual" blessings, let alone "outer" ones, when the conditions for granting them are not sound. On the other hand, the New Testament does not withdraw the promise, nor do the writers lessen the expectation, that God is moved by prayers of petition. Moreover, the one who prays is also changed. That is most obvious in the case of Paul, who discovered the grace and power of God in new ways. By acknowledging God as the one who gives us all things (cf. 1 Tim. 6:17) and by asking God for those things which God knows we need, we look out upon the world with new eyes and see ourselves as beneficiaries of a gracious God who cares for all that he has made and "is able to do far more abundantly than all that we ask or think" (Eph. 3:20). And by asking for forgiveness, we are reminded of the need to forgive others.

Christians tend to idealize the past, particularly the era of the New Testament. That era, it seems, was the golden age when heaven and earth were near to each other and when divine powers were readily available for implementation on earth in prophecies, spiritual direction, and miraculous deeds. But now, in an expanded universe, the powers from on high seem to be higher and more remote.

It is true that there is a difference, a very great difference, between the world of the New Testament and our own. Easter and Pentecost do not happen every day, and prophetic speech is not heard in every gathering for worship. In the matter of prayer in particular one can see a difference. In some portions of the New Testament, expectations about prayer—about what it can do—jar us because they seem unrealistic.

But there are different kinds, and different levels, of expectations of prayer in the New Testament. Expectations concerning the coming of the kingdom of God and the Parousia of Christ, for which Christians pray in invocations, are never abandoned even though they are modified somewhat in respect of the timing of their fulfillment. Expectations concerning the well-being of others, for which Christians pray in intercessions, are high, but it is recognized that sometimes the response of God is not exactly what has been expected and that the results are not always identical to those for which people have prayed. And expectations for oneself and one's community, for which petitions are made, are encouraged to be very high indeed, but certain parts of the New Testament readily grant that God does not always give what is requested and that one must not ask for things contrary to the will of God. When the full data are observed, it becomes clear that the distance between the world of the New Testament and our own is less than one would suppose if one limited oneself to the few choice texts that have tended to become the church's "canon within the canon" in regard to prayer. The church prefers those passages which promise the most. But by ignoring other passages it may be that the church goes too far in emphasizing the difference and the distance between the world of the Bible and our own. The result is that some people begin to think that the world in which prayer is effective is over.

But a more sober assessment of the New Testament evidence about prayer can instruct and inspire the church of today, as well as individual Christians. Prayer is not always efficacious in the way that the one who prays desires. That is illustrated in the New Testament itself, so it is not simply a modern conclusion based on an antisupernatural or skeptical world view. The challenge of the New Testament in regard to expectations concerning prayer places us precisely where we belong: in the company of those earliest Christians, suppliants before God, who prayed for the consummation of all things, for the good of all the children of God, and for a meeting of their needs and their communities' needs so far as this was pleasing to God. Expectations must indeed be high, or our prayers are unworthy, for prayer must have an urgency commensurate with the belief that God is living, active, caring, and responsive. But it is true to the witness of the New Testament to realize that a living, active, caring, and responsive God also has an agenda— and is more than an equal partner in the divine-human encounter.

In dealing with the matter of expectations concerning prayer in the New Testament, we have focused rather narrowly. One should not get the impression that prayer in the New Testament consists solely or even mainly of invocations, intercessions, and petitions. There is so much more: adoration, thanksgiving, blessing, and praise. And these form the larger context for the kinds of prayer discussed here. They are uttered and sung in response to the abundance of God's glory, grace, and power—the abundance of which the Baal Shem Tov (1700–1760), founder of the Hasidic movement in Judaism, once spoke:

> God's abundance fills the world at all times . . . and it always seeks a channel through which it may descend unto men. If our words of prayer . . . are concentrated upon God, they unite with His abundance and form the channel through which it descends upon the world.[6]

NOTES

1. Ferdinand Hahn, *The Worship of the Early Church,* trans. David E. Green (Philadelphia: Fortress Press, 1973), 20.

2. Cf. George F. Moore, *Judaism in the First Centuries of the Christian Era: The Age of the Tannaim,* 3 vols. (Cambridge: Harvard Univ. Press, 1927–30), 2:212–13.

3. Quoted from *Josephus,* trans. H. St. J. Thackeray et al., 10 vols., Loeb Classical Library (Cambridge: Harvard Univ. Press, 1966–81), 1:371.

4. These figures are based on the demographic research of Bruce W. Frier, professor of classical studies at the Univ. of Michigan, as reported in *Michigan Today* 17/4 (December 1985), 1–3. His study will be published in vol. 11 of the Cambridge Ancient History (forthcoming).

5. Quoted from the trans. by A. E. Taylor in *The Collected Dialogues of Plato,* ed. Edith Hamilton and Huntington Cairns (New York: Pantheon Books, 1961), 1372.

6. Quoted from David M. White, *The Search for God* (New York: Macmillan Co., 1983), 127.

Three

PRAYER IN THE EARLY CHURCH
Carl A. Volz

PRAYER AS DISCIPLINE

The earliest reference to the daily private devotions of the early Christians is in the *Didache*, which states, "Do not pray as the hypocrites [Jews], but as the Lord directed in his gospel (Matt. 6:16)." Then the author suggests that the Lord's Prayer (with the added doxology) be prayed three times daily (8.2). This practice soon became the normal expectation for all the faithful. The prayer was to be prayed at the third, sixth, and ninth hours, based upon the Jewish prototype following Daniel's practice (Dan. 6:11). In Acts we find these hours sacred, as when Peter and John went up to the temple at the ninth hour, "which is the hour of prayer" (3:1), and when Cornelius experienced his vision at the same hour (10:30). Peter went to his housetop to pray at the sixth hour (10:9), and it was at the third hour that the disciples were gathered for prayer at Pentecost (2:15). Tertullian devotes an entire chapter in his treatise *On Prayer* to the expectation that prayer will be said at these hours, and he encourages the faithful to observe the hours as a discipline:

> These facts are stated simply without any commands about the practice, yet it would be a good thing to establish some standard which

will . . . compel the remembrance of prayer, as it were compulsory at times to drag one away from affairs to such duty. (*On Prayer* 25)

There was considerable reciprocal influence between the hours of private prayer and the later monastic hours of Terce, Sext, and None. After A.D. 200 it was the general custom to meditate on the successive phases of Christ's passion at these hours. Hippolytus (ca. 200) offers a detailed description of the hours of prayer, which he says were observed by Christians "of old": "If you are at home, pray at the third hour and praise God, but if you are elsewhere and that hour comes, pray in your heart to God" (*Apost. Const.* 62.2). At this hour, he says, one should focus attention on Christ's crucifixion, for it was at this hour that the shewbread was offered, and Christ fulfilled this Old Testament type.

As to the sixth hour (midday), Hippolytus writes,

> Pray also at the sixth hour, for at that hour Christ was hanging on the wood of the cross, the daylight was divided and it became darkness. And so let them pray a prayer identifying themselves with the cry of him who prayed and caused all creation to be made dark. (62.4)

Regarding the ninth hour (three o'clock in the afternoon), he suggests,

> And at the ninth hour also let prayer be protracted and praise be sung that is like to the souls of the righteous glorifying God who does not lie, who remembered his saints and sent to them his Word to enlighten them. For in that hour Christ was pierced in his side . . . and fulfilled the type of his resurrection. (63.5)

Even though physical night is approaching (Good Friday evening), a bright dawn is also approaching through the waters of Holy Baptism (the vigil of Easter).

By the end of the second century, Christian discipline called for prayer at midnight as well. Tertullian offers as an argument against marriage with a pagan the difficulties encountered if a Christian woman arises to pray at midnight "when a slave of the devil is at her side" (*To My Wife* 2.4). Hippolytus is less rigorous: "If your wife is present, pray together, but if she is not yet among the faithful, pray alone. Do not be lazy about praying" (41). As the *Didache* suggests, these hours usually included the Lord's Prayer.

In addition to praying at the three fixed hours and midnight, Christians were encouraged to pray upon rising and to remember at that hour the resurrection of Christ from the grave and their own future resurrection. Christians continued, besides, the Jewish practice of prayer before mealtime. Tertullian suggests that the sign of the cross be made before meals, and he believes prayer should be said before bathing: "It is fitting for the faithful not to take food or go to a bath without first interposing a prayer" (*On The Crown* 3).

Tertullian and Hippolytus are witnesses to the discipline of prayer as observed in North Africa and Rome in A.D. 200. A contemporary, Clement of Alexandria, speaks of observing the fixed hours of prayer, but he sees a danger in merely following the letter of the law. He devotes book 7 of his *Stromata* entirely to prayer and suggests that the perfect Christian (Gnostic) devotes his or her whole life to prayer: "Not in a specified time or selected temple or on certain festivals or days, but during one's entire life the Christian in every place . . . acknowledges his gratitude for the knowledge of the way to live. We cultivate our fields praising; we sail the seas hymning" (7:7). Clement is a witness to the widespread custom of the regular five times of daily prayer, but he suggests that prayer must be continuing and constant, or as later writers put it, the practice of the presence of God.

The second century's discipline of set times for daily prayer became normative in later centuries, with the major difference that in the imperial church after Constantine what had been a private devotional practice became a form of public worship. By the time of Chrysostom (A.D. 400) one of the chief functions of the clergy was to officiate at the public services marking the fixed hours of prayer. Chrysostom complains that all too often clergy are found asleep for the early morning or late evening office. It is true that the times for private prayer became the norm for monastic practices, but monastic practices also served as models for private devotions, in consequence of the "monasticization" of the church in the medieval period.

Prayer in the sense of discipline (*askesis*) was seen as a struggle against demons and our own self-will, and so it served as a means toward the end of mortifying the flesh, whatever other benefits might accrue. Tertullian compares prayer to a battle:

> Prayer is the bulwark of faith, our defensive and offensive armor against the enemy who is watching us from every side. So let us never proceed unarmed: by day let us remember the station, by night the vigil.

> Beneath the armor of prayer let us guard our emperor's [God's] standard. (*On Prayer* 29)

A clear statement of patristic attitudes toward prayer can be found in the catechetical instructions given to baptismal candidates, for whom the obligation of prayer was stressed. In his first address to the catechumens, Cyril of Jerusalem (ca. 346) compares prayer to a race that requires the disciplined use of the mind and thoughtful reflection: "Let us brace our minds, concentrate our souls, prepare our hearts. The race is run in matters of soul, and the prize consists of rewards in heaven" (*Prologue to the Catechetical Lectures*).

The constant references by patristic writers to the necessity of prayer suggests that there was incomplete acceptance of the regimen of prayers five or seven times each day. Indeed, the repetition of the exhortations suggests that the early Christians were not heroic in their prayer life. Gregory of Nyssa's earliest extant sermon (ca. 365) complains that "the present congregations need instruction not on how to pray but on the necessity of prayer to begin with," a need that "has not yet been grasped by most people. In fact, the majority of men grievously neglect in their life this sacred and divine work which is prayer."[1] He scolds his hearers for doubting prayer's efficacy. He deplores the craftsman who "leaves prayer aside and places all his hopes in his hands," viewing prayer as lost time that could better be spent applying his craft.

For many in the early church the efficacy of prayer was thought to depend on adequate preparation. Moral preparation was believed necessary for efficacious prayer. Humility, reverence, and a sincerity of purpose were seen as safeguards against ritualism and magic. Since human wickedness can alienate God, Tertullian enjoins a ceremonial washing of hands before prayer, not because this rite is effectual but because it is a symbol of the cleanliness of the heart as one approaches God. One should be "pure of fraud, murder, violence, sorcery, idolatry, etc. This is true cleanliness" (*On Prayer* 13:17–19). Furthermore, the prayer must be accompanied by a "procession of good works." Tertullian's disciple Cyprian suggests that "prayer is ineffectual when it is offered to God as sterile. Quickly do those prayers ascend to God which the merits of our works urge upon him" (*On The Lord's Prayer* 32.63, 33.62).

Origen, Gregory of Nyssa, and Theodore of Mopsuestia repeat the same theme. Origen writes,

> It is impossible to obtain such requests if one does not likewise pray with certain dispositions and with a certain kind of faith, and a record of life lived in such and such a way. For he who prays will not obtain remission of his sins unless he forgives from his heart his brother who has offended him and asked his pardon. (*On Prayer* 8.1)

It is possible to trace the idea of moral preparation for effective prayer to Greek religions, where piety had to precede petition, but more likely it reflects Old Testament examples. The God of the Old Testament clearly connects the efficacy of prayer to moral uprightness and to the existence of a proper relationship between the one praying and God. Origen bases his ideas on the conditional nature of the fifth petition of the Lord's Prayer ("And forgive us . . . as we also have forgiven others"). Cyprian bases his concept of the necessity of piety before prayer on the account of the sacrifices of Cain and Abel, where Cain's sacrifice was acceptable owing to his moral rectitude. But it seems that the fathers derive the conditional nature of prayer primarily from the fifth petition and support it with the example of the unforgiving servant (Matt. 18:23–35) who was treated as he had treated others. They consequently suppose that apart from prayers concerning forgiveness, only prayers issuing from clean hands and a pure heart can be expected to ascend unto the Lord's holy hill (Ps. 24:4). This attitude assumes that God can be influenced by piety and good deeds, a notion much under suspicion in later Christian tradition. But associating sincerity of intent and moral purpose with prayer was a guard against a magical understanding of it. Furthermore, when prayer is defined as a sign of our relationship with God, the assumption is that there is a relationship with which to begin. One can easily identify with a person who is more inclined to converse with a friend than with an enemy. As Jesus himself said, "Not everyone who says to me 'Lord, Lord,' will enter the kingdom of heaven, but only those who do the will of my heavenly Father" (Matt. 7:21).

THE LORD'S PRAYER

For the theologians of the early church, the Lord's Prayer was the supreme model of prayer. Cyprian maintains that in this prayer, "there is absolutely nothing passed over pertaining to our petitions and prayers" (*On Prayer* 9.34). All the fathers who speak of prayer take this as their starting point. Tertullian writes that the Lord's Prayer is the base on which a "superstructure" of other petitions may be built. To be "mindful of the precepts, lest we be as far from the ears of God as we are from the precepts" (*On Prayer* 10), we should first pray Christ's prayer and then add further supplications. Tertullian suggests that by praying the Lord's Prayer first, we gain God's attention and give our personal petitions greater efficacy. This appears to be the reason that the prayer was included in the canon of the mass, as close as possible to the words of institution themselves. Origen refers to the Lord's Prayer as a *hypogrammos,* a writing copy or guide for making letters. Gregory of Nyssa suggests that all our vain desires and foolish requests will be excluded if we use this prayer as our model. Theodore of Mopsuestia affirms that correct prayer will ask for the same things as does the Lord's Prayer and thus exclude selfish and harmful things. Clearly these fathers do not mean that the simple words of the prayer contain all useful petitions, but it is in their interpretation of the various petitions of the Lord's Prayer that they explicate the meaning or content of prayer in general. It is through their own exegesis of this prayer, colored by their theological predilections, that the prayer becomes normative for them. In other words, the "norming" nature of the prayer does not produce a common understanding of the petitions; these are as varied as the theologies of the Christian communities and the theologians who interpret them. (At the same time the prayer does offer broad bounds within which interpretation must take place. Consider in this regard Origen, who believed that some Christians were sinless but who was compelled by the prayer's fifth petition to reckon with the concept of forgiveness.)

The variety of the understandings becomes evident when we compare interpretations of selected petitions. "Thy kingdom come" was commented upon most frequently. The New Testament writers gave the "kingdom" an eschatological nuance, and this direction was followed by Cyprian and Tertullian, who reflect the expectation of Christ's immediate return. Tertullian interchanges this petition with the third, so that the order is God's name, his will, his kingdom. Ernest Evans comments that this was no slip of memory but a conscious rearranging of the petitions to coincide with Tertullian's ascending order from present to future.[2] First we must subject our flesh in this world to the will of God in order that the consummation of the age may come. Given this understanding, it is illegitimate to pray for the prolongation of the present world or even, possibly, for such temporal benefits as may mitigate the evils of the present life: "How do certain persons ask for what they call a prolongation for the world, when the kingdom of God, which we pray may come, is directed toward the consummation of the world?" (*On Prayer* 5.10). Cyprian also sees in this petition the hope for a future as yet unrealized in the present: "We do well in seeking the kingdom of God, that is, the heavenly kingdom" (*The Lord's Prayer* 13.276.6). This eschatological understanding of the second petition decisively influenced subsequent exegesis in the Latin tradition.

Theodore of Mopsuestia represents an advance on this view. While giving the future kingdom its due, he holds that an awareness of the eschatological kingdom should inform present ethical behavior and human-divine relationships. By this time (5th cent.) the imminence of Christ's return had receded in importance, and to think of God's kingdom was now to "think on things that are congruous to the heavenly citizens." This is in keeping with Theodore's strongly ethical bent and his Antiochene Christology that stressed the humanity of Christ and the reality of the incarnation over against the docetic tendency of Alexandria.

Origen completely ignores eschatology and locates the kingdom of God within us. In this petition the believer asks "that the kingdom of God might be established and bear fruit and be perfected in himself" (*On Prayer* 25.1). By nature all humans live in this world under either Satan's rule or Christ's, so the prayer for the kingdom is to ask that we be translated from the rule of Satan to the rule of Christ. Gregory of Nyssa repeats Origen's basic theme: "God's kingdom is . . . the absolute lordship of God in the world; its 'coming' is its penetration into the present affairs of men."[3] It is redeemed human existence.

Given the variety of interpretations, how did the Lord's Prayer serve as a limiting norm? In all the examples above, the "kingdom" represented the highest and the best to which humans could attain, whether in the future or the present. To pray for anything less was inadequate or even sinful. Tertullian says one should not pray for the continuation of the present evil age. Others understood the "kingdom" as the gift of likeness to God as a reflection and foretaste of the future age.

The fifth petition, "Forgive us our sins," exercised a powerful influence on the doctrines of sin and humanity, especially when some theologians were reluctant to acknowledge the sinful state of humans. Tertullian writes that "a request for forgiveness is a confession of guilt, because he who seeks forgiveness confesses guilt" (*On Prayer* 7.185.25). In his other writings, Tertullian stresses the necessity of confession prior to the reception of baptism (*On Baptism* 20), but he believes that after the confession of one's sins (and the implied absolution) it is possible to attain perfection in this life. Not sinfulness but perfection is to be the rule for Christians, and when one is guilty of "sin" there is available the "second plank" of forgiveness through public confession and absolution. Tertullian does not explain why one must continue to pray for forgiveness (in the Lord's Prayer) after baptism.

Origen understands debts, or transgressions, as duties to perform before God: "We owe debts in that we have certain duties not only of giving but also of speaking what is right. We are obligated to have a certain disposition toward others" (*On Prayer* 28.1). He further states that it is possible so to discharge one's debts as to be free of them. If that is not done, there is a statute of limitations beyond which the debt is automatically canceled. For Origen confession of sin is not an essential element of prayer, because perfection in this life is attainable for the gnostic Christian.

After baptism the believer is to maintain a state of holiness. In this, Origen follows his predecessor, Clement of Alexandria:

> The fact is that Clement's Gnostic is presumed to be as near perfection as is possible for one who is still in the flesh. He knows God, and this knowledge is virtue. There is little wonder then, that confession of sin will have but an insignificant place in the Gnostic's prayer.[4]

Origen understands sin primarily as ignorance, and it is this which leads to the transgression of rules. In effect he prays, "Forgive us for being human like everyone else, and give us the strength to become holy here and now." Gregory of Nyssa offers a similar view of sin and finds the means for canceling it not in the expiatory sacrifice of Christ but in the second clause of the prayer, in which sin is remitted by forgiving others.

In Cyprian we find a basically different view of sin, as expressed in his commentary on this petition. Among the fathers he stands as a lone witness to the serious nature of sin and guilt and to its enduring presence:

> How necessarily, how prudently, and how salutarily are we admonished that we are sinners by being compelled to make petition for our sins, so that while forgiveness is asked of God the mind is recalled to a sense of its guilt. Lest anyone should be self-satisfied as though innocent . . . we sin daily. (*On Prayer* 22.52)

Cyprian aside, the idea of Christian perfection among many early theologians, especially in the East, precluded the existence of sin among the baptized. Confession had little place in their life of prayer. Confession played no part in early liturgies, including those of North Africa. The Lord's Prayer exercised a normative influence by reminding the church to come to terms with the nature and existence of sin despite attempts to ignore it or explain it away.

THE CONTENT OF PRAYER

Origen suggests that a model prayer for daily use should

(*a*)   praise God through Christ and the Holy Spirit;
(*b*)   thank God for blessings we have received and enjoy;
(*c*)   recognize one's sinfulness;
(*d*)   request forgiveness of sin;
(*e*)   ask for great and heavenly gifts for all people, family and friends and ourselves; and
(*f*) praise God through Christ in the Spirit.

Thus all prayer is to begin and end with doxology or thanksgiving. The requirement of doxology appears to take precedence over other forms of prayer in these early writers, "for this is our first delight as creatures" (*On Prayer* 33). Gregory suggests that we ought not rush into God's presence before acknowledging his greatness and giving thanks for gracious gifts of the past, present, and future. Tertullian says that "to honor God" is the Christian's first duty in prayer, and if the angels are continually singing, "Holy, Holy, Holy," we humans can do no less (*On*

Prayer 2, 3). He writes that we rise at midnight to praise God for his wondrous deeds and to thank him for his mercies. The doxological nature of prayer became the raison d'être for early Christian monasticism; as Benedict's Rule puts it, "Let nothing take precedence over the praise of God." Origen's third and fourth categories have to do with the forgiveness of sins, but in fact he does not dwell on this as a regular aspect of prayer.

Intercessory prayer is Origen's fifth category, which he defines as "request to God for certain things made by one who has greater confidence" (*On Prayer* 14.2). That is, primarily the "perfect" and the saints have a hearing with God, and intercession is the work of the Spirit: "The apostle rightly assigns intercession to the Spirit as being superior and having confidence in him to whom he addresses himself" (*On Prayer* 14.25). Gregory in his homilies on prayer makes no reference to intercession, probably because intercession is for him not a prerogative of the average Christian. The notion that only the heroic believer ought to intercede is related to the prayers of the martyrs, who by virtue of their impending death had a special entrée to God. One thinks here of Perpetua, who prayed for her brother who had died a pagan; the answer she received was that he had been admitted to heaven. Perpetua was a young woman who died in the persecution of Lyons in A.D. 177. She received a vision that informed her that her prayers had been answered, presumably because of her anticipated martyrdom. This is the earliest recorded instance of the efficacy of prayers for the dead in the Christian tradition, but praying for the dead is a dubious practice with a long and troubled history in the church.

The early Christians prayed for others, especially for the government and rulers, for persecutors, and for the needy. Clement of Rome prays for "all in distress, the poor and sick, the hungry and those astray, that all people may recognize that you alone are God and that Jesus Christ is your divine Son and your people the sheep of your fold" (*1 Apol.* 59). Intercessory prayers form part of all the early liturgies; for example, Justin (ca. 160) insists that prayers be offered to God for all who are in need, and by the fourth century, when Cyril of Jerusalem wrote, intercessory prayer was a regular part of the eucharistic liturgy.

Origen, in another list of the contents of prayer, includes "supplication, which is offered by someone who needs something" (*On Prayer* 14.2). Gregory suggests that we first make supplication for spiritual things such as wisdom and faith, and only then, if necessary, "descend" to physical needs, which he calls childish toys. Augustine appears more balanced in his treatment of prayer. In his "Letter to Proba," he says one should pray for happiness, which includes good health, safety, the physical necessities of life, and the welfare of children and friends. It is even proper to ask for positions of rank and authority for ourselves and families, provided we do so in order to help others and not out of pride. He offers the Stoic golden mean as the ideal:

> Give me not riches or poverty, but only what is necessary for life. Sufficiency is not to be coveted for its own sake, but to provide for bodily health and clothing, in accordance with our personal dignity, making it possible for us to live with others honorably and respectably.[5]

Reading through collections of early Christian prayers, one seldom finds petitions for physical needs, and even expositions on the fourth petition tend to become spiritualized, with "daily bread" referring to the Eucharist. For this reason, Cyril of Jerusalem began the practice of including the Lord's Prayer in the eucharistic liturgy. But early Christians were very much concerned for the physical well-being of those in need, as witnessed to by the practice of weekly distribution of food and clothing, together with the alms that had been brought by the faithful at the offering. The association of these physical goods with the intercessions that followed seems to indicate a concern in prayer for all in need, believers and nonbelievers alike.

Origen, following John 16:23, insists that prayer be made in the name of Jesus: "[The Father] will give it to you in my name." Christ is the supreme advocate with the Father, without whom one cannot approach God: "One must not offer a prayer to the Father apart from [the Son]" (*On Prayer* 15.2). Christ is the high priest by whose death we are reconciled to the Father and now live in a new relationship. The work of Christ as high priest is continuous and will not be completed until the final consummation. Gregory develops the theme that only through Jesus do we possess the grace that is assumed in prayer, and Cyprian repeats the theme of Christ's intercessory role. The earliest collects terminate with prayer "through Jesus Christ, in the Holy Spirit."

Patristic prayer is also focused on the community rather than on the individual. This is reflected in statements that address "our Father." Theodore of Mopsuestia writes,

> I do not wish to say my Father but our Father, because He is a father
> common to all in the same way as His grace, from which we receive
> adoption of sons, is common to all. In this way you should not only offer
> congruous things to God, but you should also possess and keep fellow-
> ship with one another, because you are brothers and under the hand of
> one Father. (*Catechetical Homily* 11.7)

Prayer belongs to the church alone, and even when Christians pray
alone in private they do so as members of Christ's body, and as such
offer petitions for the welfare of that body. Each Christian's private
prayer is a single note that contributes to the grand harmony of the
church. Cyprian comments that we are not asked to pray, "Give me this
day my daily bread," and one does not ask to be delivered from evil for
oneself alone. "When we pray, it is not for one person, but for the entire
people, because we the whole people are one" (*Lord's Prayer* 8). He
goes on to give examples of the three men in the fiery furnace and of
the disciples after the ascension, who found and expressed their unity
in the apostles' doctrine, fellowship, the breaking of bread, and prayer
(Acts 2:42). In Tertullian's cryptic language, Unus Christianus, nullus
Christianus ("A Christian in isolation is no Christian").

Agnes Cunningham's statement can serve well as a summary:

> [The early understanding] of Christian prayer is [as] an activity by
> which a disciple of the Lord, with him and through him, seeks God in
> faith, intercedes with God in hope, experiences and communes with
> God in love and filled with the Spirit of Jesus, reaches out in concern
> and service to others. . . . Christian prayer as understood and taught by
> the fathers, was essentially christological, biblical, ecclesiological.[6]

NOTES

1. Gregory of Nyssa *The Lord's Prayer,* in *Ancient Christian Writers,* ed.
Hilda C. Graef (New York: Newman Press, 1954), 18.21.

2. Ernest Evans, "Introduction," in *Tertullian's Tract on Prayer* (London:
SPCK, 1953), xiv.

3. Georg Walther, cited by Robert L. Simpson in *The Interpretation of Prayer
in the Early Church* (Philadelphia: Westminster Press, 1965), 100.

4. Eric G. Jay, *Origen's Treatise on Prayer* (London: SPCK, 1954), 30.

5. Agnes Cunningham, *Prayer: Personal and Liturgical,* Message of the Fathers of the Church 16 (Wilmington, Del.: Michael Glazier, 1985), 114.

6. Ibid., 31.

PART TWO

UNDERSTANDING PRAYER

Four

PRAYER IN THE OLD TESTAMENT: CREATING SPACE IN THE WORLD FOR GOD

Terence E. Fretheim

What great people is there that has a god so close to it as the Lord our God is to us, whenever we call upon him? (Deut. 4:7)

Your iniquities have made a separation between you and your God . . . so that he will not hear. (Isa. 59:2)

Closeness and distance. That is the way it is with relationships. They are not static, always and everywhere the same. What those in relationship do with and to each other inevitably has an effect upon the nature of the relationship. What happens is commonly expressed in the language of closeness and distance. We have all said of persons in relationship, "They are not close anymore." Or, "She seems so distant whenever she's with him." We refer not to spatial, but to relational distance. Such distance has the capacity of reducing the possibilities for fullness of relationship on the part of one party or both. For example, if one person in a relationship gives the other the "silent treatment," the other cannot be a spouse or a parent or a friend in the way she or he wants to be. The silence reduces the possibilities (for growth, communication, healing) within the relationship.

So it is in many ways with divine-human relationships, as the texts cited above make clear. The distance or separation occasioned by iniquity does not mean that God has moved to another part of the globe; it is a distance *within* relationship. The relationship is thus not what God wants the relationship to be. God is not able to be the kind of God that God wants to be. God's possibilities within the relationship are more limited. More specifically, lack of communication makes a difference in what is possible for God within the relationship. "I was ready to be sought by those who did not ask for me . . . . I spread out my hands all the day to a rebellious people" (Isa. 65:1). Greater closeness in the relationship as manifested in communication would thus make a difference in God's possibilities in the relationship. In other words, prayer gives God more room in which to work, makes God more welcome, creates more relational space (less distance) for God.

I believe that the use of this image of closeness and distance is of much help in our efforts to elicit the Old Testament understanding of prayer. But first of all, we note some general presuppositions that seem to underlie the Old Testament understanding of prayer. We then move to a few passages that support our theme of prayer as creating openings (relational space) for God in the world. Finally, we explore some texts relating to the repentance of God, texts that are especially illustrative of this theme.

PRAYER AND RELATIONSHIP

Fundamental to any talk about prayer is an understanding of the nature of the relationship between God and world, more particularly, between God and the human. Generally speaking, *prayer is an aspect of the gift of relationship that God has established with us.*

1. At the heart of the matter, the relationship between God and the human is of such a nature that God and human beings can meaningfully interact with one another. God can speak to the human, and the human can understand the Word spoken and can respond in kind, knowing that, in turn, God can hear the human and respond. The Old Testament understands that this possibility is given with creation; it is not something peculiar to the chosen people. This might be said to be at the center of the meaning of the image of God (Gen. 1:26–28), though on occasion prayer language is used of animals (Ps. 147:9; Joel 1:20). The specific language of prayer is used to describe the worship activity of non-Israelites (see Isa. 16:12; 44:17, 20; Jonah 1:5), but an evaluation is also given: they "keep on praying to a god that cannot

save." At the same time, God may answer the prayers of such people (see Jonah 1:14; 3:8–10). Prayer for enemies or for non-Israelites is also attested (e.g., Jer. 29:7; Ps. 109:4).

2. Speech is an integral aspect of the divine-human relationship. Other ways of interacting with one another might be cited, but speaking and hearing, listening and responding, are central to what it means to be in relationship (with the heart as well as the lips and mouth, Isa. 29:13). From the creation stories on, conversation is perhaps the most prevalent way in which God and humankind relate to each other. The absence of such conversation, of listening and responding, is a sign that the relationship is not healthy, and is an occasion for divine wonderment (Isa. 50:2) and a prelude to judgment (see Jer. 35:17; Isa. 65:12). Samuel's ceasing to pray for his people is considered to be a "sin against the Lord" (1 Sam. 12:23; though see Jer. 11:14). The new heaven and the new earth will be characterized by intimate divine-human conversation (Isa. 58:9; 65:24).

3. The Old Testament does not speculate on *how* such conversations take place. It only testifies to the reality of such experiences. Individuals do hear God speak, in both direct and indirect ways, through such "vehicles" as dreams, visions, and "personal" appearances. Divine speech is never understood to be unambiguously divine, but it is commonly *believed* to be from God and sufficiently clear and effective to shape faith and life.

4. The divine-human conversation is genuine conversation. It is not only God who speaks to the human; humans speak to God. It is not only humans who respond to divine speech; God responds to human speech. The relationship thus has a fundamental integrity to it. It is not only what God says that affects the relationship; what human beings say affects the relationship as well. *For the sake of a genuine relationship, God so enters into the world and relationships that God is not the only one who has something important to say.* The human has the God-given capacity to affect the nature of the relationship in both positive and negative ways. God is thus pictured in the Old Testament as both delighting (as well as rejoicing) in response to the human conversation and being provoked to anger. (It might be noted here that, for such varied responses to make sense, one must speak of divine temporality; God is not always delighting or always angry.)[1]

5. By establishing such a relationship with human beings and giving

them the capacity to function as a true party in that relationship, God makes himself vulnerable. People can now speak words to God that hurt—words that reject his Word, words that presume upon the relationship, words inimical to the continuance of a harmonious relationship. Those in relationship become more vulnerable the more they collapse the distance between them, the more they share of themselves. God's "homing" in Israel means for God a greater vulnerability. Yet that is a risk that God is willing to take for closeness.

6. Because the God who is in relationship with us loves us, this God is desirous of close communication with us. In the language of Prov. 15:8, "The prayer of the upright is God's delight." God wants people to pray. Indeed, God is delighted when people pray. It is a sign of health in the relationship when such communication lines between God and humankind are open. Prayer is one of the ways in which the relationship can be kept close. On the other hand, when people do not pray it is a sign that something is not right in the relationship; it is not as close as God wants it to be.

PRAYER AND GOD'S POSSIBILITIES

We now need to take a closer look at certain texts within this framework. Isaiah 65:1-2 pictures God in agony over the absence of prayer on the part of those whom God loves:

> I was ready to be sought by those who did not ask for me; I was ready to be found by those who did not seek me. I said, "Here am I, here am I," to a people that did not call on my name.

When we do not pray, it hurts God. Even in the absence of prayer, however, we see here a God who remains eager for communication. "I spread out my hands all the day [even] to a rebellious people" (Isa. 65:2).

Such lack of communication makes for distance between the parties in the relationship. Even more, such *silence on the part of the people means that God is not able to be God for them in a way that God would like to be.* This would be comparable to how silence on the part of a child or spouse affects the possibilities in relationship for a parent or the partner in marriage. So, too, God's possibilities are limited by the lack of responsiveness on the part of the people in the relationship. Isaiah 59:1–2 puts it well:

> Behold, the Lord's hand is not shortened, that it can-
> not save, or his ear dull, that it *cannot* hear;
> *but* your iniquities have made a separation between you
>   and your God,
> and your sins have hid his face from you so that he
>   *will not* hear.

Human sin and the lack of responsiveness within the relationship can adversely affect the way in which God can be God to people. Distance affects what is possible for God, not theoretically in terms of whether God can hear or work at all but in the particularities of a given situation, where God can be so shut out that God's presence is less felt and less effective. In honoring the integrity of the relationship, God is less able to bring God's power to bear in a given situation. People do have the power to give God less room in which to work in their lives, to close down a situation to God's possibilities to a greater or lesser extent. Hence, *what is possible for God in responding to prayer in a way that is in the best interests of all concerned may vary from one situation to another.*

A variety of other passages could be cited in this connection. The people's sins drive God away from the temple (Ezek. 8:6), from that more intensified form of divine presence in Israel. Because the people "have made their deeds evil," God "will hide his face from them *at that time*" (Micah 3:4; cf. Deut. 32:19–20; Isa. 57:16–17). Second Chronicles 15:2 (cf. 12:5; 24:20) indicates that the divine forsaking is a response to human forsaking. God's presence is not a "forced entry"; indeed, human wickedness can push God back along the continuum of presence so that it becomes less intense and hence less effective. Virtually all the prophetic references to divine hiddenness relate issues of divine presence in relationship to human wickedness.

One of the results of this distancing is that God will not hear, let alone answer, prayer (see Ps. 66:18; Prov. 1:28). The absence of justice is especially cited in this connection:

> When you spread forth your hands,
>   I will hide my face from you;
> even though you make many prayers,

I will not listen;
your hands are full of blood.
(Isa. 1:15; cf. Zech. 7:8–13)

Fasting like yours this day will not make your voice to
be heard on high
[for you do] not share your bread with the hungry, and
bring the homeless poor into your house.
(Isa. 58:4–7)

This increasing distance would appear to make for an intensification of divine presence of another sort, namely, wrath (see Jer. 33:5). Yet the images seem to function differently. The movement away *is* a movement of wrath (Isa. 54:8); wrath is a distancing. The people can have their own way, with all its consequences. The result is that Israel's enemies flow into the "spaces" left by the divine withdrawal (see Isa. 64:7; Jer. 12:7; Ezek. 39:23). On the far side of hiddenness, in eschatological vision, the intensity of the divine presence pours into Israel's life once again (Ezek. 39:29). But between now and the eschaton, prayer is a way of trying to deal with those "spaces," that is, of making more room in life (through, e.g., repentance) for the more intense forms of the presence of God.

The psalms, too, speak of an anguish over the divine absence because of sin (see Psalms 38; 74:1; 89:46; Lam. 5:20) and wonder about the length of the absence and the seeming finality of it. A few texts (e.g., Job 13:24; Ps. 22:1) question the divine absence in the face of causes unknown. Yet in every such instance, while God's presence *to* Israel is diminished in its intensity, God's presence *for* Israel remains alive and well, though that may be hidden from the people's eyes (e.g., Psalm 44). The God of promise is so desirous of closeness that God will always be working toward the fullest possible intensification of presence and all that that means for the salvation of God's people. (Short of a given of creation, namely, epistemic distance, "no one can see God and live.")[2]

It should be made clear that God is constantly taking the initiative and does "break through" in special intensifications of presence from time to time. First Samuel 3 witnesses to a highly perseverent God, unsurpassed in working for, creating, and finding openings even when all the doors seem to be closed. But human prayer, even if no more than a "Speak, Lord, for thy servant hears," will make a difference in what is possible for God in any given situation. God is now more welcome, given more room to be present and at work. Such human openness provides another "lever" with which God can be more effectively present and at work. Prayer makes a difference to God. "And Samuel lay until morning; then he opened the doors of the house of the Lord" (1 Sam. 3:15).

PRAYER AS GOD'S POWER SHARING

This discussion needs to be related to the fact that any relationship of integrity will entail a sharing of power. There can be no true relationship if one party has all the power. This is something that God has built into the very created order of things (see Gen. 1:26–28): God's first words to the newly created are power-sharing words. God has hereby entered into a power-sharing relationship with the human (though not in such a way that one cannot speak of God's power apart from such relationships). God has chosen not to do everything in the world unilaterally. *While God does not finally let go of any situation, God has chosen not to be the only one in the world with power.* But what the creature does with the power at its disposal will affect how God is able to use God's power in a given situation. Prayer is a way in which the power at the disposal of the human can be more in tune with the will of God, and they can act together rather than competitively. In a nutshell, *prayer is a means that God can use to extend or expand on God's possibilities.* Yet this is done in a way appropriate to the power-sharing relationship that has been established. Thus, for example, no matter how open to God a given situation of illness may be, surgeons will still be needed. The will, insight, and energy of the human are combined with the power of God.

Let it be noted that an intelligible account of what happens on such occasions can be given apart from faith for a variety of purposes, for example, those of medical research. But the biblical faith would claim that *no full account of any event can be given without factoring God into the process.* And prayer has to do with that which brings the human and the divine factors into the fullest possible power-sharing effectiveness. Prayer makes more room for God to be present and to do God's work: "Israelite prayer tends to make the believer an energetic co-operator and not a beatified enjoyer of God."[3]

Passages that relate prayer (especially intercession) and the repentance of God may now serve to illustrate these matters in especially forceful ways.

That the repentance of God is a difficult theme is evidenced not least in the way in which the matter has been ignored in biblical scholarship. I suspect, however, that the neglect of such a common theme (forty explicit references) is due less to the theme's difficulty than to the theological perspectives of the commentators. The fact of the matter is that this theme has been incorporated into Israel's most common credal statement in its latest two (of ten) instances: "The Lord our God is gracious and merciful, slow to anger, and abounding in steadfast love, and repentest of evil" (Jonah 4:2; Joel 2:13). Both cases occur in prayer contexts, as do most other usages of this theme.

God repents of *evil*. God is never said to have committed any sin of which God needs to repent. To repent of evil is to turn from an announcement of judgment, the effects of which, if forthcoming, would make for less than total well-being (and hence, evil). The theme is also used in connection with God's turning away from wrath (cf. Ps. 106:40, 45, which roots the divine turning in "the abundance of his steadfast love"). The divine repentance is forthcoming (*a*) in response to the prayer of the people (see Jonah 3:10), (*b*) in response to the prayers of an intercessor (see Exod. 32:14), or (*c*) in response to a human situation but with no apparent human mediation (see Jer. 42:10).

Repentance is sometimes represented as a continuously available divine possibility. As Jer. 18:7–9 states,

> If *at any time* I declare concerning *a nation or a kingdom*, that I will pluck up and break down and destroy it, and if that nation, concerning which I have spoken, turns from its evil, I will repent of the evil that I intended to do to it.

This divine possibility stands in sharpest contrast to any arbitrariness of divine action. Rather, it reflects the extent to which God is willing, and indeed eager, to go in order to fulfill God's uncompromising will for the salvation of as many as possible. God's constant openness to repentance stands in the service of this divine unchangeability (in connection with which the phrase "God does not repent" is used; cf. Num. 23:19).

This passage in Jeremiah 18 (as well as the Book of Jonah) makes it clear that Israel has no monopoly on this divine possibility. Because God's will is for the salvation of the whole world, God will repent of judgments upon the repentance of any people. God in fact does this for Israel (see Jer. 26:19) and for non-Israelites (see Jonah 3:10). This divine repentance is available not only before the judgment is exacted but also after the judgment is already in progress (see Joel 2; Jer. 42:10).

This passage (and others) also makes it clear that, regardless of whether conditional language is used, virtually all announcements of judgment are subject to divine repentance. The exceptions are those related to the eve of the fall of Samaria (Amos 8:11–12) and of Jerusalem (Ezek. 7:4, 9). In the latter context we even see God forbidding Jeremiah to intercede in behalf of the people (11:14; 14:11–12), believing that it is only through judgment that life will once again be possible. But normally the situation is open for the divine repentance, because for God, if salvation is at all possible, that takes priority over even a word that God has spoken. Thus we have to conclude that often God does not want prophecies to be fulfilled, precisely so that God's salvific will can be realized. In such cases, it would seem, God's will is done when prophecy *fails!* It should be noted in this connection that Jeremiah 26:2–4 (and other passages) makes it clear that God is not certain regarding what Israel will do in response to the prophetic announcement. The only way the integrity of these announcements can be maintained is if God does not finally know what Israel's response will be, however much God may be said to be aware of all the possibilities. People's prayers (in these cases, of repentance of sin) thus have the capacity of shaping not only the future of the people but also the future of God.[4]

INTERCESSORY PRAYER

We now turn to those texts which speak of God changing direction in view of human intercessory prayer (see 1 Sam. 12:23; Num. 14:19–20; Joel 2:17–18). The two key texts having to do with intercession on which we would like to focus are Exod. 32:12–14 and Amos 7:3–6. Note that the intercessor does not suggest that God's announcement is unjustified or inappropriate; the judgment is deserved. Nor are Israel's

60

Terence E. Fretheim

good deeds appealed to. But reasons to repent are offered to God: (a) God's reputation among non-Israelite peoples; (b) God's reasonableness; (c) God's promises; and (d) the weakness of Israel.

What status do such reasons have for God? It seems clear that without the prayers of the intercessor, the results would have been other than what they were. The prayers do make a difference, not simply for the people but for God (many comparable references could be cited with respect to petitions—e.g., 1 Kings 21:27–29; Isa. 38:1–6; Jer. 26:19). It also seems clear that God is not now being given data that were previously unavailable to God. The only difference is that certain matters are now being forcefully articulated by one with whom God has established a special relationship. Because God honors the relationship, the decision-making situation is changed from what it was prior to the prayer.

Through such prayers the human party in the relationship enters into the decision-making sphere set into motion by God's announcement (cf. Gen. 18:17–19; Amos 3:7). The two are now together in a power-sharing situation with respect to the shaping of the future. God now has some new ingredients with which to work. The decision (will), insight (knowledge), and energy of the intercessor are placed in the service of God. God thus has more possibilities within that situation (both the situation of the intercessor and that of the ones for whom intercession is made) with which to work. And if those human beings, upon whom God has chosen to be dependent in other ways, think in these ways, then they take on a significance for the future that they do not have when treated in isolation by the divine mind. *God honors what the individual brings as an important ingredient for shaping the future.* The situations are now more open, for both God and human are working together. It means that God's presence is more intense and hence more effective. The possibilities for the future are more extensive.

A cautionary word needs to be voiced here. God's responsiveness could be narrowly related to Israel's prayers, and the relationship conceived in mechanical or external or formal or quid pro quo terms. One must insist on the living, dynamic character of the relationship and those involved in it. Responses within any relationship, even between those who know each other very well indeed, are not as predictable as one might think. Moreover, the pervasiveness of evil in the world can get in the way of God's response to prayers. Just the complexity of the causes that feed into any moment in life prevent one from tracking possible connections between prayers and potential responses to prayers. Factors such as these should stop us from reducing these matters to absolute clarity or from thinking that by our prayers the future can be shaped with precision. One must also reckon with issues of divine power and the way in which God has chosen to work in the world in response to prayer. Thus, for example, God may well be deeply involved and God's will for the positive resolution of the issue may be clear, but the accumulated effects of sinfulness may be such that they are beyond God's power to control, given the self-limited way in which God has chosen to work in the world.

An analogy may be offered: human sinfulness has occasioned numerous instances of the misuse of the environment. Some of that misuse, for example, radiation, asbestos, pesticides, has caused cancer in human beings. Human beings may be forgiven the sin for such, but the effects of their sinfulness continue to wreak havoc upon people's health. We confess that in response to prayer (and in other ways) God is at work in this evil, struggling to bring about positive results. But one must also speak a "Who knows?" (Joel 2:14) or a "Perhaps" (Jonah 3:9) with regard to the effect of that divine work upon this generation of people. It is not a question of whether God wills good in the situation. It is rather the question of what can in fact be done and how and when, given God's own self-limited ways of responding to evil in the world.

To conclude, prayer may be said to be a God-given way for God's people to make a situation more open for the God who desires to be as close to people as possible and who always has their best interests at heart. *Prayers do shape the future in ways different from what would have been the case had no prayers been uttered.* And this is because of the kind of God to whom the prayers are spoken. The God who is revealed is not one who is unbending or unyielding, one who assumes a take-or-leave-it attitude. The people of God are not in the hands of an iron fate or a predetermined divine order. God is open to taking new directions and changing courses in view of the interaction between God and people. Yet always in view will be God's salvific will for all. That will, which no prayers can affect (and which hence one ought not pray to change), will remain unchangeable.

The people of God have been given the power of prayer by their God as a means (not unlike preaching; cf. Rom. 10:14) in and through which God works to accomplish God's purposes in the world. In different words, prayer is one way in which the mission of God can be furthered in the life of the world—even beyond the range of our voices.

NOTES

1. See my *The Suffering of God: An Old Testament Perspective* (Philadelphia: Fortress Press, 1984), 39–44.
2. Ibid., 66–67.
3. Edmond Jacob, *Theology of the Old Testament* (New York: Harper & Bros., 1957), 176.
4. On this, see my *The Suffering of God*, 45–59.

Five

THE GOD OF PRAYER
Paul R. Sponheim

THE REALITY OF GOD AND OUR REALITY

We begin with what seems undeniable: that prayer is human. Prayer is part of human reality. We eat and drink, we work and play, we are born and we die . . . and we pray. Prayer has a remarkably tenacious hold on the human. Earlier in this century one might have predicted that as enlightenment spread, prayer would fade from our lives as surely as the rising sun's rays penetrate even the thickest forest. This does not seem to be happening. Prayer is resilient, as is suggested by the new wave of spirituality engulfing us. Funny things happen to people on the way to godless worlds: they pray. Consider this remark by Anthony Kenny:

> One thing seems clear. There is no reason why someone who is in doubt about the existence of God should not pray for help and guidance on this topic as in other matters. Some find something comic in the idea of an agnostic praying to a God whose existence he doubts. It is surely no more unreasonable than the act of a man adrift in the ocean, trapped in a cave, or stranded on a mountainside, who cries for help though he may never be heard or fires a signal which may never be seen.[1]

The grim desperation in this passage tells us something more about the human reality of prayer: that prayer depends on the reality of that

63

which is not human. It depends on the other, the transcendent. Prayer depends on God. Prayer is a cry to God—a cry of pain, of praise, of petition. But in every case it is a cry to God.

Indeed, in speaking *to* God, prayer is perhaps that part of our life which most clearly speaks *of* God. If there were no God, Christian service would still reach a good goal in feeding the hungry and housing the homeless. Perhaps the beauty of Bach and of soaring Gothic arches would bless the human scene even if their making were wholly human. Prayer resists such reduction. Here an either/or rises to meet us. How shall we turn toward one who is not there, one who is not *anywhere*? There may be powerful forms of autosuggestion, but prayer is not one of them. If we did not believe in God, we might turn to such human realities as the power of positive thinking. But the dialectic of that activity would be different. We would be turning only to another aspect of ourselves. There would be no place for genuine surprise through interaction with an other; there would be no energy there other than our own. People who pray do not suppose they are having to do only with themselves. And so we must speak of God if we propose to understand prayer.

The logic of prayer leads us to speak to God, but that speaking is hardly untroubled. The problem is twofold. It is not clear that we must speak of God in order to understand ourselves and our world. It is not clear that there is something left over to talk about when we have explained what we experience as selves in the world without talking of God. Yes, there is the stubborn reality of prayer, and the churches crumble more slowly than we might expect. But we believe we know how it is that things happen in reality. We can trace causal sequences in humankind and nature. We believe this, as Rudolf Bultmann argued in his demythologizing program, as surely as we go to work day after day. In view of how we understand the nature of reality it is not clear that we can speak of God.

Or if we must speak of God, it is because we must speak against God. It is not just that the world is not perfect. The degree of evil, its clear-eyed intensity, seems to speak of that which is more than human. But what does it say? Robert Scharlemann has put it this way:

> No single series of occurrences in the twentieth century has so demanded a second language besides that of human agents, intentions,

and actions as has the Holocaust. What happened cannot be adequately told by a narrative whose subjects are human beings, political forces, and national entities. Something "supranormal" occurred. But it is not clear what that second language can be. Some authors (Richard Rubenstein, for example) think it calls for the negation of theological language: that is to say it does call for saying something about God, but what it calls for is that God was not there and perhaps is not at all.[2]

We must speak of God. We cannot speak of God. Or if we can, we can only speak against God. These sentences do not go well together in any paragraph. Yet that is precisely our task: to write them together in the story that is our living, our praying, our thinking. One can understand why our prayer so often is, "I believe, help Thou my unbelief!" God's reality and our reality—that is our theme.

GOD IN RELATIONSHIP

If we must speak of God, what shall we say? Three things, I believe.

First, that God is other than we are. God is not merely "another other" (as we are to each other) but qualitatively other or inherently superior to us. The logic of prayer makes this clear. You can love your spouse, your country, perhaps even your enemy . . . and your God. You can work for your family, for humankind in a broader sense . . . and for God. In these activities God is not singled out; the difference seems a matter of degree. But we pray only to God. Here God stands alone.

Thus we speak of God as different in kind from us. We speak of God's power, but we do not ask whether God could break Walter Payton's career rushing record in the NFL. We refer to God's knowledge and wisdom, but we do not connect divine knowledge and wisdom with the range of intelligence measured by the Graduate Record Examination. What we are getting at in this difference is that God's very being is different from ours. The difference is, as we say, ontological.

One way of speaking of that difference is illustrated by the Christian doctrine of creation. God is the creator of all being that is not God. That which is not God is made by God; only God is eternal. And the making is truly radical; it is not the shaping of matter. We are made—so the doctrine goes—"out of nothing." There is a difference of kind here, and the difference abides. That which is made by God is real, but its reality is of another kind from God's reality. We are not made out of God but are made by God out of nothing.

God is other than we are. When we pray we know this. We would not pray to one of us—as much as we may admire and respect one another. We want the church in its faithful thinking, in its faith seeking understanding, to speak of God as other. And the church has done that. There is a great tradition of otherness called the *via negativa*. Note the negatives: God is unchanging, nontemporal, invisible, immortal, and the like. God is not as we are.

The difficulty with such speaking is that it becomes difficult to see how the God spoken of can connect with such beings as we are. The very power of such speaking threatens to carry God far away from us. A God who is other becomes a God who is distant and, perhaps, finally a God who disappears.[3] Even by an act of the imagination it is hard to conceive how such a God could have to do with us. For we are beings who laugh and cry, who work and struggle. How can a being who cannot change weep or struggle? How can a being who is simply nontemporal work toward an end? We want to speak of the otherness of God, but such speaking seems to separate God from us. Or does such speaking simply turn against itself? Does the logic of faith lead to silence? Does faith become sheer, unknowing trust? Is the truest prayer precisely "silent" prayer? Is the highest knowledge of God to know that we do not know?

What of other ways of speaking of God's otherness? One such way is to speak of God as omni: omnipotent, omnipresent, omniscient, for example. Such a God is clearly other than we are, for we make no such claims for our power, knowledge, or presence even in our most prideful moments. But does this way of speaking represent the centrifugal tendency to alter or abolish the relationship that prayer requires? It depends. It depends on whether or not that of which we speak can sensibly be said to be shared. Does God's having all of something require that we have none of that?

Knowledge, presumably, can be shared. There may be radically individualized aspects of knowledge, but there is also sharing in knowing. A mother and a father "know" their son's suicide differently, of course, but they do know it together. And there can be radically differing degrees of knowing that are not competitive, that do not threaten one another. If Albert Einstein were my physics teacher, he might still be said to know (nearly?) everything about the formula $E = mc^2$ without suggesting that my partial knowing were not real knowing.

With power it seems to be different. Of course power can be shared. In the United States we speak of a "balance of powers" in the government. Marriage partners work at power sharing. But then no one party does indeed have all the power. Our third term, presence, comes quickly to mind here. Is there presence without power? If we continue to speak of God as having all the power there is, can we meaningfully speak of God's presence *with* us? Can God be said to be everywhere present, everywhere powerfully present, without being said to have all power?

These questions await further treatment. But we have run ahead of ourselves. In beginning this section, I said we must say three things of God. The first is that God is other. It has become clear that we have difficulties in saying that. We have such difficulties precisely because we want to say a second thing: God is with us, God is for us.

God is with us and God is for us. The logic of prayer requires this as surely as it requires that God be other than we are. If we did not believe God were for us, or at least that God *could* be for us, we would not pray. And it will not avail to say that God is for us, if God is not with us— here, in our living and struggling. Karl Barth protested against liberal theology's loss of the otherness of God. But he knew God's freedom was the freedom of the gospel:

> The God of the Gospel is no lonely God, self-sufficient and self-contained. He is no "absolute" God (in the original sense of the absolute, i.e., being detached from everything that is not himself). To be sure, he has no equal beside himself, since an equal would no doubt limit, influence, and determine him. On the other hand, he is not imprisoned by his own majesty, as though he were bound to be no more than the personal (or impersonal) "wholly other." By definition the God of Schleiermacher cannot show mercy. The God of the Gospel can and does.[4]

At the heart of the Christian faith is the figure of the crucified One. Barth is right. When we look at the cross, what do we see? We see suffering and death. And when we look to the cross we look to God. What kind of a being can hang on a cross? That is the question we must ask. Or perhaps the fuller question is, What kind of a being can hang on a cross and in doing so make a difference for all of humankind and all of human history? Our speaking of God must be normed by the center of faith, and that is, of course, the person and work of God in Jesus of Nazareth.

For that matter, even our other speaking of God suggests that God is with us and for us. A God who is with us and for us is in some sense (of which more must soon be said) like us. So we speak of God as personal, even though we do not thereby suggest that God is an individual person in just the sense that we are. But when we speak of God as personal, we do mean to say that God knows and feels, that God chooses and acts. Similarly, even the language crafted to register God's otherness seems to link God with us. To say that God is everywhere present is to say that God is present—and we know what being present means. To say that God is all-powerful (or everywhere powerful?) is to say that God has power to act and does act—and we know what it means to act. This God who is other is at the same time like us.

That is the third thing we seek to say in this first effort at talking about God in relationship: the otherness and the relatedness of God are to be held together. God is other and, to be God, does not need to be in relationship to what is outside God. Thus the divine Trinity indicates living relatedness within God's own self, in contrast to our situation of knowing relationship in dependence upon external others. So it would not be meaningless to speak simply of God, even though it would not be clear how *we* could do so, if God were not in relationship to us. But we speak here as Christians, and so we speak not simply of God but of God in relationship.

Yet we speak of *God* in relationship. A God who is with us and for us may indeed be like us, but that God is still other than we are. God has not stopped being God by becoming God for and with us. It is this we must understand if we are to understand prayer. In prayer we draw close to God, or we pray because God is close to us and draws us. Closeness does not remove mystery. In prayer we speak to someone we cannot see and we do so by means that we cannot chart within our normal scheme of causes. We believe we can do so and we believe we must do so, because we believe God is other than we are. Otherness and relationship: these two are together in prayer. To speak of how they are together a second discussion is needed.

GOD IN RELATIONSHIP:
A SECOND DISCUSSION

This discussion is second in a double sense. It not only follows the first, it depends on the first. First we sought to say *that* God is both other and related. Now we ask *how* this is so and how it may be understood to be so. The fundamental theme we will develop is that in relationship, God's power is freely limited and God's will is faithfully realized.

This relationship roots, of course, in God's will to create. We have already spoken of how the triune God as eternal is limited by no external other. But God chose not to remain alone. God chose to create that which is not God. And the crown of that other-for-God is the human, whose very freedom images the freedom of God the Creator. But it is not an isolating freedom. It is with the human, in particular, that God seeks a relationship of love and trust. If God had created us so that we merely felt free but were actually determined in our response, God would have known (even if we did not) and the relationship would have been spoiled. To grant only the illusion of freedom would be to trivialize the relationship by denying the possibility of willing commitment in the face of known risk on both sides.

Søren Kierkegaard well understood the amazing logic of a God who actually seeks a reciprocal relationship with the creature. I present the passage as Kierkegaard wrote it, with apologies for what we now recognize to be noninclusive language:

> O wonderful omnipotence and love! A human being cannot bear that his "creations" should be something directly over against him; they should be nothing, and therefore he calls them creations with contempt. But God, who creates out of nothing, who almightily takes from nothing and says "Be!" lovingly adds "Be something even over against me." Wonderful love, even his omnipotence is under the power of love! . . .
>
> Thus love, which made a human being to be something (for omnipotence let him come into being, but love let him come into being over against God) lovingly demands something of him. Now that is the reciprocal relation.[5]

Sin comes in not as part of God's creation but as a perversion and usurpation of it. God's response to sin indicates that God's freedom is at work in God's faithfulness. God acts freely to create the other. And again, God acts freely to re-create—to save—the other.

Again too, in this action God chooses self-limitation. That is the point of the beautiful Christ hymn of Philippians 2, where the talk is of the divine *kenosis*, or emptying. Surely this is God's choice; no one forces this upon God. In this emptying there is freedom. Yet the freedom yields genuine limitation. One can distinguish between two kinds of limitation. First, God is bound by God's commitment. Again it is Kierkegaard who puts this as well as anyone. He contrasts the incarnation to a king who merely pretends to be a servant in order to win a maiden's love. Notice particularly the point that this genuine limitation by which God must and does love is precisely a testimony to the difference in kind or superiority in principle of which we spoke in the previous section:

> God's servant-form is . . . not a disguise, but is actual; not a parastatic body, but an actual body; and from the hour when he with the omnipotent resolve of his omnipotent love became a servant God has so to speak imprisoned himself in his resolve, and now must go on (to speak foolishly) whether he wills to or not. He cannot then betray himself. There exists for him no such possibility as that which is open to the noble king, suddenly to show that he is after all the king—which is no perfection in the king (that he has this possibility), but merely discloses his impotence, and the impotence of his resolve, that he cannot really become what he desires to be.[6]

God can become what God wills. And God did that in a willing of one thing that is indeed purity of heart. Clearly here God's will is faithfully realized. God wills to love us to the end, and nothing can separate us from that will. As 2 Timothy has it, "If we are faithless, he remains faithful—for he cannot deny himself" (2:13).

In limitation in this first sense God's will is indeed realized. It is made real in the flesh and blood of the Son's love. But there is also limitation in a second sense. Once again God creates freedom, now not from nothing but from the negative of sheer opposition to God. God works powerfully to set free, to give faith, to "call, gather, enlighten, and sanctify," as Luther said. But that love can be rejected is written in the sands of human history and in our lives as well. Thus that sure sign of God's love, that seal set upon the heart of God, Jesus, can speak in anguish of his forthcoming rejection at Jerusalem:

> How often would I have gathered your children together as a hen gathers her brood under her wings, and you would not. (Luke 13:34)

What structures have theologians of the church used to speak of God's action in the world? Traditional Lutheran dogmatics speaks of God as "preserving, concurring in and governing" the free action of that which is not God.[7] I want to direct attention particularly to the divine concurrence. Thus Christian faith does indeed speak of God as the Alpha and the Omega. God is at the beginning and the ending of every event. The freedom of that which is not God is preserved, and it is judged or governed. But in between there is the middle in which God is at work *and* we are at work. This is not to say that God works just as we do, as an agent external to other agents. God is still the Creator and has access to the creature(s) in ways other creatures do not. But this God who acts "first" and "within" is still the one who as Creator gives freedom and so seeks to work in the middle through the means of the creatures. And it is just there, in the middle, that our prayer takes place.

GOD IN RELATIONSHIP TO PRAYER:
THE ART OF THE FUGUE

Because it is this God to whom we pray, our prayers are powerful. Given the relationship of which we have spoken, things happen because of prayer. These effects can be distinguished: (1) We are affected. (2) God is affected. (3) The world is affected.

1. So far I have written more of God than of us. Perhaps that is not a grievous sin. But of course we are affected by our relationship with the God of whom I have written. This is a general truth of our being, but prayer as a direct and conscious focusing of the relationship reveals this truth with particular and distinctive emphasis. Perhaps the point can be made most fundamentally in this single sentence: In prayer we come to know who we are. And who are we? The answer has both an ontological and a moral ring. We are creatures, dependent for our very being on the one to whom we pray. We are sinners, needing to come clean about our sin against the one to whom we pray. We are servants, blessed with life and forgiveness and directed to our neighbors near and far. Ann Belford Ulanov, an analyst, has written about ways the person who prays is set free from self-preoccupation:

In prayer, we re-collect ourselves and feel touched by what or who we
know ourselves to be. We recover a sense of ourselves, now
disidentified somewhat from the different roles we take on during each
day. For finally in prayer, I am I, for better or worse, before God, and not
mother or teacher or wife or lover or some identity I share with my de-
pressed or anxious or dulled feelings.[8]

2. God is affected by our prayers. Surely it is clear from what I have
said in the preceding section that God's very life is affected by what we
do. I have spoken of Jesus' sorrowing word over Jerusalem: I would,
but you would not. What we do does matter *to God*. There is joy in
heaven over one sinner who repents. Perhaps people of faith have always believed this. Theologians, however, have not always been very
helpful in any attempt to understand it. Caught up in trying to render
the otherness of God, theologians have neglected the ways in which
humankind can affect God. In fact, the writings of the theologians
have spoken extensively of God's impassibility. Happily, a corrective is
discernible. Thus Jürgen Moltmann, drawing on Abraham Heschel's
sense of divine pathos, says,

> Granted, the theology of the early church knew of only one alternative
> to suffering, and that was being incapable of suffering (*apatheia*), not-
> suffering. But there are other forms of suffering between unwilling suf-
> fering as a result of an alien cause and being essentially unable to suffer,
> namely active suffering, the suffering of love, in which one voluntarily
> opens himself to the possibility of being affected by another. There is
> unwilling suffering, there is accepted suffering and there is the suffering
> of love. . . . The justifiable denial that God is capable of suffering be-
> cause of a deficiency in his being may not lead to a denial that he is inca-
> pable of suffering out of the fullness of his being, i.e., his love.[9]

It would be bizarre to say that God can experience only pain and not
joy. Rather, our prayers of praise, adoration, and thanksgiving rightly
recognize God's transcendent relatedness to us and are received by
God accordingly. Such praise matters to God. When we lament, that
matters to God. Both matter. There are suffering and joy in heaven. But
the point to be emphasized here is that God is indeed enthroned on the
praises of Israel (Psalm 22) and, we may believe, on our praise as well.
Thus perhaps praise and adoration are in fact the most fundamental of
all forms of prayer, for thus one simply recognizes God as God. Such

praise seeks nothing in particular for itself. It fulfills itself outside itself—in God, as it sings, "Let God be God."

Adoration and praise may be the most fundamental forms of prayer, but clearly petition is the most problematic. A first form of petition, that of seeking something for oneself, is perhaps not so hard to understand as it is to practice rightly. There is, on the one hand, the reality of change in the one praying. But what is the objective side of the subjective effect? Consider, for example, a prayer for forgiveness. Such a prayer appropriately recognizes our condition: we have sinned against God and we do need forgiveness. By seeking forgiveness we do not compromise the fact that Christ has already died for the sins of all. We seek the realization of what is founded in Christ, the realization of that gift in the living, contemporary relationship with God. Martin Luther put it this way:

> Here again there is great need to call upon God and pray, "Dear Father, forgive us our debts." Not that he does not forgive sin even without and before our prayer; and he gave us the Gospel, in which there is nothing but forgiveness, before we prayed or even thought of it. But the point here is for us to recognize and accept this forgiveness.[10]

It is not particularly difficult to understand how this works, if we remember that it is the living God to whom we pray. In the living relationship that is prayer the person praying receives assurance of God's forgiving presence. This is difficult to understand only if one is determined to reduce all communication to the modalities of touch, sight, and hearing. At a level more fundamental to our humanity we do indeed "taste" the forgiveness of God freshly, and we know that it is sweet indeed. Similarly, the person praying for strength and guidance in the life of service experiences the responding presence of God. A direction is made clear. We are turned toward the other and come to understand needs and possibilities in a way impossible for a self turned in upon itself. Things become as clear as they need to be. We are not, after all, talking and listening to a computer. We are talking in freedom with a person of freedom and a person who is truly other than we are.

3. What shall we say of changes in the world beyond changes in the person praying? This is probably the most difficult aspect of prayer for us to understand. There are, of course, those changes which occur in the world through changes in the person praying. If we are changed by

our praying, our world will not go unchanged. Much could be written of that, noting that such liberation theologians as Dorothee Soelle, Leonardo Boff, and James Cone—and indeed, Loren Halvorson—do not fail to claim the resource of prayer.[11] But the space that remains for me must be devoted to the more difficult topic of intercessory prayer. Clearly this is an important part of our praying. How may we understand what takes place in and through such prayer?

Any change in the world beyond ourselves will depend on God; that is clear. We pray to God. How might our prayers make a difference to God in such a way that they come to make a difference in the world? We might suppose that we pray to change the will of God. Our prayers do sound like that sometimes. But I have already stressed the Christian understanding that the will of God is ontologically sure. To pray to change the will of God is ontologically futile. God is in charge of God's will and God has already willed one thing. Even God cannot change that.

Moreover, I wonder if it is not religiously wrong-hearted to pray to change the will of God. If God's will is for the salvation and blessing of all, for example, it is not the will of God that needs changing. Lament shares the pain of life with God in sharp tones fitting the pain, it is true, but it does so within the context of trust in God. If Jesus could pray, "Not my will, but thine be done," so surely should we. The action of God serves the will of God in the back-and-forth of the relationship between God and humankind.

Do we pray, second, to change the knowledge of God? In the simplest sense we cannot, of course, add to the knowledge of God. Surely God knows all that we know. But there may be a sense in which our prayers do bring freshly to God's attention matters already known to God. As prayer draws together aspects of the actual world, it is itself actual and it is known newly by God. Prayer says "thou" or "you" to God. It brings the matter prayed about into the very life of God with the intensity of address. God not only hears what we pray but that we pray and how we pray. In some such way we may struggle to understand the importunate widow; we may come to see that our prayers do affect the knowledge of God.

Most important, intercessory prayer adds to the power of God by which God works in the world. In the preceding section, I spoke of how God acts in "concurrence with" human reality. May not prayer be just such a secondary cause? Surely prayer is itself a kind of energy, of concern. It is an instance of reaching out toward the person or situation for whom or for which we pray. That prayer is heard by God, by the God who is the continuing creator active in every situation in the universe. As God hears that prayer, God judges the prayer by the standard God's sure will provides. Then in whatever measure is appropriate God draws on that prayer in working within the situation for which the prayer is intended. That situation is itself some mixture of necessity and possibility; it is a situation of relative or finite freedom. In such freedom God's will may not be done, but God will be at work in that continuing situation.

Why might one choose to speak of prayer as the art of the fugue? I am thinking of how the fugue combines a constant theme with a wide range of variations and developments, overlapping motifs, and changing keys. Surely the music of our praying is the art of the fugue. This is true of our intercessions. We intercede with confidence, because we know what the will and work of God is. We can appropriately teach our children how and what to pray. But we often do not know exactly what will work for blessing and salvation in specific situations. We pray then with Reinhold Niebuhr for the wisdom to tell the difference in our praying between the things that cannot be changed and those that should be changed. We seek to accept our own responsibility even as we pray.

We are glad that the Spirit intercedes for us. We are glad that God judges our prayers, that God distinguishes between wants and needs, even when we do not. And we are glad that God is the master musician who plays the fugue with us and in us. We believe God plays well, following the score set in the salvific will of God and improvising as is needed in the performance that our cacophonous universe represents. Believing this, we know what we need to know. And so, hearing a melody, we gladly take up our instruments and lift up our voices.

NOTES

1. Anthony Kenny, *The God of the Philosophers* (Oxford: At the Clarendon Press, 1979), 129.

2. Robert P. Scharlemann, *The Being of God: Theology and the Experience of*

Truth (New York: Seabury Press, 1981), 122. See also Arthur Cohen, *The Tremendum* (New York: Crossroad, 1981).

3. See the thorough discussion in Langdon Gilkey's *Naming the Whirlwind: The Renewal of God-Language* (Indianapolis: Bobbs-Merrill, 1969). Cf. Frederick Sontag, *Divine Perfection* (London: SCM Press, 1962), 83–125.

4. Karl Barth, *Evangelical Theology: An Introduction*, trans. Grover Foley (New York: Holt, Rinehart & Winston, 1963; Garden City, N.Y.: Doubleday Anchor Books, 1964), 8.

5. Søren Kierkegaard, *Samlede Vaerker*, ed. A. B. Drachman, J. L. Heiberg, and H. O. Lange, 15 vols. (Copenhagen: Gylendals, 1901–36), 10:132–33 (trans. mine). Cf. the trans. of *Christian Discourses* by Walter Lowrie (Oxford, 1939), 132–33.

6. Søren Kierkegaard, *Philosophical Fragments*, ed. H. V. Hong, trans. David Swenson (Princeton: Princeton Univ. Press, 1962), 44.

7. Heinrich Schmid, *The Doctrinal Theology of the Evangelical Lutheran Church*, 3d ed. rev., ed. Charles A. Hay and Henry E. Jacobs (Minneapolis: Augsburg Pub. House, 1875, 1899), 171.

8. Ann Belford Ulanov, "What Do We Think People Are Doing When They Pray?" *Anglican Theological Review* 60 (1978): 388.

9. Jürgen Moltmann, *The Crucified God*, trans. R. A. Wilson and John Bowden (New York: Harper & Row, 1974), 230.

10. Theodore Tappert, ed. and trans., *The Book of Concord* (Philadelphia: Muhlenberg Press, 1959), 432.

11. See, e.g., Dorothee Soelle, "We Do Not Know What We Should Pray," in *The Truth Is Concrete*, trans. Dinah Livingstone (London: Burns & Oates, 1969), chap. 10. Cf. Leonardo Boff, *The Lord's Prayer: The Prayer of Integral Liberation* (Maryknoll N.Y.: Orbis Books, 1983), and James Cone, *God of the Oppressed* (New York: Seabury Press, 1975), esp. chap. 8, "Divine Liberation and Black Suffering."

Six

PEOPLE OTHER THAN CHRISTIANS PRAY
Paul Varo Martinson

To God belong the east and the west and wheresoever you turn there is the Face of God. Truly God is All-pervading, All-knowing. (Koran, Surah of the Cow, 115)

Grant me, Lord, to know and understand which is first—to call on thee or to praise thee? and again, to know thee or to call on thee? For who can call on thee, not knowing thee? For he that knoweth thee not may call on thee as other than thou art. Or is it better that we call on thee that we may know thee? (Augustine *Confessions*, opening lines)

Those who lovingly devote themselves to other gods and sacrifice to them, full filled with faith, do really worship Me though the rite may differ from the norm. . . . For it is I who of all sacrifices am recipient and Lord, but they do not know Me as I really am. (Bhagavad-Gita 9.23–24)

For from the rising of the sun to its setting my name is great among the nations, and in every place incense is offered to my name, and a pure offering; for my name is great among the nations, says the Lord of hosts. (Malachi 1:11)

People other than Christians pray. Does that really matter for Christians? It is hardly possible today to consider Christian prayer without at the same time taking this fact about others into account. But how might we do so, and to what purpose? We will ponder that question,

even though it may not be answered easily; we must ponder, for to fail
to do so risks treating Christian prayer as if within a Christian ghetto.
"The integrity of every religion is at stake in its awareness of them all,"[1]
for to ignore the neighbor—and every religion is now neighbor to all
religions—implies the disquieting prospect of a faith irrelevant to the
world. A Christian community in deliberate isolation is no Christian
community.

But how broad is the scope of our question? It is one thing to ask it of
Jewish and Muslim prayer. With Jewish prayer, we do not have much
trouble. Indeed, we ourselves use the Jewish Psalter, and we acknowledge the Jewish people (even now!) as somehow the "covenant
people"—following Paul in that—even though Jesus has been rejected
as Israel's messiah by rabbinic Judaism. The Muslims do not rate as
"covenant people" in our thinking, or at least not yet, though the Muslims lay claim to the Abrahamic heritage.[2] The Koran's rejection of
Jesus as crucified and risen Lord and divine Son—though it does recognize Jesus as Israel's messiah—is a rejection that is as firm and
unshaking as the Jewish.

But the scope of our question is widened immeasurably when the
entirety of non-Semitic faiths is brought before us. What shall we do
with Hindu, Buddhist, Taoist, Shintoist, Sikh, Native American, African, Zoroastrian, Mormon? The list gets long. Idolaters abound out
there; heretics abound; denials of Jesus as Christ and denials of God
abound. Can we do other than mourn or laugh at such foolishness?

Yes, we must, for Scripture does.

LET ALL THAT BREATHES
PRAISE THE LORD

In breath we all share. Our common share in breath invites us to
community in prayer: "Let all that breathes praise the Lord" (Ps. 150.6;
cf. Psalms 19; 148—where all things animate and inanimate are summoned to praise). How could it be clearer?

While in breath we all share, yet in prayer we are apart. In prayer we
experience the immunity of faiths—Jew from Muslim, Christian from
Hindu. Is that as it should be? Does the Muslim summons to prayer
summon us also?

> God is most great. God is most great.
> God is most great. I witness that
> There is no god but God; I witness that
> There is no god but God. I witness that
> Muhammad is the Apostle of God; I witness that
> Muhammad is the Apostle of God.
> Come to prayer! Come to prayer!
> Come to the good! Come to the good!
> God is most great. God is most great
> There is no god but God.[3]

Does it summon us? No? Will it if the offending words about Muhammed are excised? Does that call then summon us? Others? Can there be community in our praying—one in a mosque, another in a temple, another at a shrine, yet another in a church or a synagogue? Is it only that, as old Shylock says, "I will buy with you, sell with you, walk with you, talk with you, . . . but I will not pray with you."[4] Yet, do we not all, Muslim and infidel, Christian and Jew, share in that one breath—"let all that breathes"? Yes indeed. Of the earth, we are also of breath, for "God . . . breathed into his nostrils the breath of life; and man became a living being" (Gen. 2:7). This is a breath that witnesses both to our glory, for we are of God, and to our mortality (Ps. 39:5, 11), for we are of earth. This breath links flesh with spirit.[5]

But do those folk out there really pray? Let us take a look at their prayers and see what we think. Many Hindus of today still pray the prayers of their ancient forebears, the Aryan peoples of northwest India. We might peek into their psalter, the Vedas, going back some two millenniums before Christ. Here we find praise to Indra:

> Who stilled the quaking of the mighty earth
> and set at rest the agitated mountains,
> who measured out the middle regions of space
> and gave the sky support: he, Men, is the Lord![6]

There is a tale to tell of how this Indra brought salvation to the cosmos ("who slew the dragon and made the seven streams to flow") and how he judges the sinner and rescues his people from their enemies:

> Who slays with his bolt, before they know it, all those that have committed great sin; who does not forgive the insolent his insolence, who slays the *dasyu* [non-Aryan], he, O folk, is Indra.[7]

Here too we find prayer to the somber Varuna, who sees and knows all:

> The mighty overseer on high
> espies our deeds, as if he were
>   quite close at hand.
> The gods through him know all men do,
> though often men contrive to act
>   all stealthily.[8]

And therefore it is right to bring to Varuna the confession of one's sin:

> If we men commit, O Varuna, an offense
>   against the heavenly ones,
> or in thoughtlessness transgress your laws,
> oh punish us not![9]

Surely there is something rather substantial to the awareness of God that these psalms express.

Lament of the innocent who suffer without cause is another theme of gentile prayers. In the song book of ancient China, the *Shih Ching*, we read,

> Oh, vast far-spreading Heaven, whom we all call parent!
> I am innocent and blameless, yet I suffer from such great disorders.
> Majestic Heaven, you are too stern; for truly I am innocent.
> Majestic Heaven, you are too cruel, for truly I am blameless.[10]

and

> The proud rejoice. The troubled are in great distress. Oh, azure Heaven!
> Oh, azure Heaven! Look upon these proud men and have pity on the
> troubled. Those slanderous men, who was it who devised their plans? I
> would take those slanderous men and throw them to the wolves and ti-
> gers. If wolves and tigers refuse to devour them, I would throw them
> into the northlands. If the northlands refuse to receive them, I would
> throw them into the hands of August Heaven.[11]

And Heaven is not silent; Heaven does act for the people. In China's most ancient theology of history, the *Shu Ching*, Heaven judges the wicked ruler of the Shang (or Yin), and covenants with another people, the Chou. In his speech King Wu of Chou declares of the king of Shang that he with strength pursues his lawless way. . . . Dissolute, intemperate, reckless, oppressive, his ministers have become assimilated to him; and they form parties, and contract animosities. . . . The innocent cry to Heaven. The odor of such a state is plainly felt on high.[12]

He has therefore cut himself off from Heaven and brought enmity between himself and the people.[13] But "Heaven loves the people."[14] And because "Heaven sees as my people see; Heaven hears as my people hear," and because Heaven's people cry out on account of injustice, Heaven hears and acts. The Shang is overthrown.[15]

The Buddhist, who denies reality to all gods, including Vishnu, Siva, Indra, Allah, Yahweh, and Heaven, in a nonpersonal sort of way intercedes with and on behalf of all sentient beings. This is prayer that has no object of address; it simply embodies an elemental movement of the heart. Is it by profound wisdom, perhaps, that the Buddhist first turns us back to breath?

With the first inhalation of the breath [at birth] there arises a desire to continue existence—the desire to invite the breath of the world of future living. . . .

Just as you have a desire to exist yourself, all other living things have a desire to exist. . . . Try to develop thoughts of loving kindness to all sentient beings around.

First begin with your home, the beings in your home. With loving kindness spread your thoughts to them. . . . Then observe those around your village, around your town, around your street. And we surely say, save all things living around my house . . . neighborhood . . . city . . . country . . . state . . . continent in which I live. May all such beings live in happiness, joy and without hatred toward each other. . . .

Then come to the lower spheres of animals. Experience the animals that are living in the world. And all animals—bless them to have that state of living, that state of peace. Try to feel them. Touch them. . . . Try to bring them round you and embrace them in your loving kindness. . . .

Go down to the lower life of the insects and the birds in the air, the fish in the seas, oceans, rivers, and lakes. And with loving kindness wish that all life upon the earth . . . be assured sanctity and peace. And in that peace experience your thoughts. Now you will learn how to be one with them. Can you experience it? Can you do it? Can you practice it? Hmm? Can you practice it? Loving kindness toward all living things? . . .

If you practice that, you will find the entire world of sentient life coming closer to you. . . .[16]

Is this, even by a Buddhist, praising the Lord? Or is it an act that, if not evil, is vain?

Does the Christian breathe his or her prayers better than does the Shi'ite Muslim, the devout of whom regularly beseech,

> He who pardons the greatest sins by His clemence!
> He who lavishes blessings by His bounty!
> He who gives abundance by His generosity!
> Sustenance to me in my adversity!
> Companion to me in my solitude!
> Aid to me in my affliction!
> Benefactor to me in my blessing!
> O my God
> and God of my fathers,
> Abraham, Ishmael, Isaac and Jacob!
> Lord of Muhammad, the Seal of the Prophets,
> and his household, the chosen ones!
> Revealer of the Torah, the Gospel, the Psalms
> and . . . the Wise Quran!
> Thou art my cave [of refuge]. . . .
> If not for Thy mercy, I would have been among the perishing,
> and Thou annullest my slip.[17]

So what do we think? Are these breathings real prayer or vain prayer? If the human spirit is there, is the divine Spirit also?

YET FOR US THERE IS ONE GOD

> For although there may be so-called gods in heaven or on earth—as indeed there are many "gods" and many "lords"—yet for us there is one God, the Father, from whom are all things and for whom we exist, and one Lord, Jesus Christ, through whom are all things and through whom we exist. (1 Cor. 8:5–6)

Is this good news or bad for those others who pray? Do all those who pray address the "one God," even if it be by many different names? Or is Allah in fact in competition with this one God; is Krishna in fact in competition with Christ?

In John 1:18 we read, "No one has ever seen God; the only Son, who is in the bosom of the Father, he has made him known." This verse might give us some clues as to how to proceed. The theme or subject of this verse is God. Concerning God two things are said. Negatively,

God is said to be without discernible attributes: "No one has ever seen God." This seems to say that the subject, God, is unavailable to us, that nothing positive can be predicated. Many kinds of mysticisms have long emphasized this kind of negative talk about God. John, however, does not stop there. The negative is followed with a positive. The "only Son" has revealed God. Therefore, through this predicate, Jesus, God is available to us. If the only thing that could be said about God were negative—that God is not seen, not heard, not known—then indeed we would hardly have cause even to discourse about God, much less to pray to God.

Jesus is the "only Son," but is he the only revelation? Hardly. For, "in many and various ways God spoke of old to our fathers by the prophets; but in these last days he has spoken to us by a Son" (Heb. 1:1–2). How many and how various are, then, these ways? In Romans 1 we find that even creation itself is a revealer of God: "Ever since the creation of the world his invisible nature, namely, his eternal power and deity, has been clearly perceived in the things that have been made" (Rom. 1:20). It will not be long, then, before we turn back to the pages of the Old Testament and there find that the vistas broaden. Indeed, even Abram is blessed by the uncovenanted, by the enigmatic Melchizedek. This Gentile "was priest of God Most High" in Salem (later Jerusalem) and is acknowledged in Scripture as superior to Abraham, for "the inferior is blessed by the superior" (see Gen. 14:18–20; Heb. 7:7 takes its cue from Ps. 110:4). The "only Son" is not the only revelation but one of many. What then is the relationship of this one revelation to the many?

The New Testament deals with this question only in a very limited way. Its main struggle is with the relation of the one revelation, Jesus, to the prior revelation to Israel. What was Jesus' relation to the covenant with Israel? This question is struggled with long and hard and receives its fullest expression in the very difficult chapters of Romans 9—11.

What, then, about the rest—those counted as Gentiles, the uncircumcised? There are strong words about being transferred from darkness to light, or from death to life, or from idols to the true God (cf. esp. 1 and 2 Corinthians, Ephesians, and Colossians). At the same time there are hints that the Gentiles and their religious traditions have a place within the divine economy, even as did Israel's past—and future.

There is a small cluster in the Pauline tradition of seldom-used words that open up some space for these considerations. We can gather these terms under the heading of forbearance.

In Acts 14:16 we read that "in past generations he *allowed* all the nations to walk in their own ways," and in 17:30 that "the times of ignorance God *overlooked*." The two sermons from which these assertions come, the first in Lystra, the second in Athens, may well not be Paul's words as such, and moreover, the key words do not even occur in Paul's letters. Nevertheless, the ideas are very Pauline. In Rom. 2:4, speaking of both Gentile and Jew,[18] Paul writes, "Or do you presume upon the riches of his *kindness* and *forbearance* and *patience?*" In 3:25 (26) again, we read that God "in his divine *forbearance* . . . had *passed over* former sins."

The general import of these verses is that prior to Christ, God's relation to the Gentiles had been a relation of grace, a relation that was to be definitively realized in Christ, and that the name of this grace is forbearance or patience. It creates a space for God's further working.

A number of things are of striking interest here. First, there is a clear effort to make a statement about the effectiveness of divine grace prior to Christ and outside Israel. To be sure, the Jews do have an "advantage" (Rom. 3:12), an advantage that is understood to be the result of a divine choosing (Romans 9). Nonetheless, this advantage is only of a preliminary sort, having a "custodial" nature (Gal. 3:24), an advantage that has its definitive completion in Christ (Gal. 3:25). It seems, then, that there is a kind of parallelism of thought. To be sure, the advantage the Jews have in the covenant is different from and more ample than the "divine forbearance" granted the Gentiles, yet grace is affirmed as characterizing God's relation to both Jew and Gentile before but in view of Christ.

These terms, it should further be noted, set forth a relation. Forbearance is not an abstract quality of God but a quality of God's relationship with people—gentile people. If in Ephesians we read that "you Gentiles in the flesh" were once "without God in the world" (Eph. 2:11–12), this certainly cannot contradict the positive relation God has with Gentiles, as these other terms establish. If on the part of the Gentiles, there is no relation to God (if they are "without God"), that simply means that they do not share in the historical covenant relationship with God, even while the relationship defined by "forbearance" was always theirs.

A third thing is to be noted in this collection of terms. They are to be taken in an active, not passive, sense. God does not sit back and take an attitude of noninterference; rather, God is actively present in the gentile world. The contexts in Acts in which the terms under consideration occur make this plain. Acts 14:16 is preceded and followed by a treatment of divine providence and revelation: "Yet he did not leave himself without witness, for he did good and gave you from heaven rains and fruitful seasons, satisfying your hearts with food and gladness." Acts 17:30 is preceded by an even more elaborate discussion, making far more daring use of Greek religious categories. Paul, according to Luke, feels compelled to cite approvingly Epimenides the Cretan, who is speaking on behalf of Zeus, making the point that the Cretans falsely claim to have the tomb of Zeus. That is false, Epimenides says, because Zeus is immortal:

> They fashioned a tomb for thee, O holy and high one—The Cretans, always liars, evil beasts, idle bellies! But thou are not dead; thou livest and abidest for ever; For *in thee we live and move and have our being*.[19]

Adding a second punch to the first, Paul goes on to cite his own countryman, the Cilician Aratus:

> Let us begin with Zeus. Never, O men, let us leave him unmentioned; all ways are full of Zeus and all meeting-places of men; the sea and the harbours are full of him. In every direction we have to do with Zeus; *for we are also his offspring*.[20]

In Rom. 2:4 (as in Acts 17:30) it is made plain that this act of divine forbearance is an active relation intended to elicit a response of faith, or "repentance," to use Paul's exact expression. This is also exactly the response intended in God's revelation to Israel.

It should, finally, be observed that this forbearance was only to be understood in reference to God's will to be gracious in Christ. Speaking to Gentiles about their incorporation into the covenantal promises through Christ, Paul writes, "Note then . . . God's kindness to you" (Rom. 11:22). Both Jew and Gentile are united in that divine intent to be finally gracious in Christ to all:

> For I tell you that Christ became a servant to the circumcised to show
> God's truthfulness, in order to confirm the promises given to the patri-
> archs, and in order that the Gentiles might glorify God for his mercy. As
> it is written,
>   "Therefore I will praise thee among the Gentiles,
>   and sing to thy name."
>
> (Rom. 15:8–9)

God's gracious forbearance shown to the gentile world opens up space
for God's continued and new work; it is a grace given in view of Christ.
Christ, in fulfilling the covenant with Israel, also opened the way of direct access for Gentiles.

We read of an altar "to an unknown god" in Athens. Paul does not
denounce this as demonic but finds a point of connection: "What . . .
you worship as unknown, this I proclaim" (Acts 17:23). Elsewhere Paul
does refer to idol worship as demonic. As Paul says,

> What do I imply then? That food offered to idols is anything, or that an
> idol is anything? No, I imply that what pagans sacrifice they offer to de-
> mons and not to God. I do not want you to be partners with demons.
> You cannot drink the cup of the Lord and the cup of demons. You can-
> not partake of the table of the Lord and the table of demons.[21]

The point, however, is not that the idols as such are demons: they are in
fact nothing. What prompts Paul to speak of them as demonic is the
practice of some Corinthians of observing both Christian and idola-
trous worship practices. This, in effect, brings the worship of God
down to the level of the worship of that which is really not God, and
that is demonic. In Galatians Paul refers to certain Jewish practices
with the uncomplimentary term of "elemental spirits" (Gal. 4:3, 8–10).
This language is used because the practices had been made obligatory
by some, thus nullifying the gospel. When something less than the
gospel is placed on the same level as the gospel, it closes up the space
for God's work and is by that very fact transformed into the demonic.
It seems to be the case for Paul that the issue does not concern the subject that reveals—does not concern whether it is really God with
which Jew or Gentile has to do—but instead concerns the attributes or
predicates accorded to that subject. "To an unknown god" is no different from saying that "no one has seen God." But that negative is not
sufficient, for "the only Son . . . has made him known." It is the predicates that the Gentiles did not know; that is what concerned Paul.

All this will have to shape our understanding of "pagan" prayer, even today. The issue is not first of all whether it is God who is being addressed in the prayer of Jews, Christians, Muslims, Hindus, Buddhists, and others, but whether God, to whom prayer is addressed, is known as God finally wills to be known—in the crucified and risen Lord Jesus.

IN THE NAME OF JESUS

The only thing that distinguishes Christian prayer from other prayer is that Christian prayer is prayed "in the name of Jesus."[22] Christians pray in this name not in order to cancel out other prayer but in order rightly to ground all prayer. That Christians pray "in the name of Jesus" means that Christian prayer takes place within the will of God that is made complete and concrete in Jesus. The transcendence that Jesus addressed as Father and that Israel confessed as the God of Abraham, Isaac, and Jacob is the same transcendent power that raised Jesus from the dead and to which Christians pray. God is decisively known here, in the events of Israel's past and in Jesus. All prayer, whether Christian or not, if it is truly prayer, finds its final justification here in this series of events from Israel to Jesus. So Christians believe.

There are two sides to this business of praying in the name of Jesus. First, the subject (God) is had by us in the predicate (Jesus)—that is, in Jesus we experience God and nothing less. Second, we are had by the subject (God) through the predicate (Jesus)—that is, through Jesus, God lays hold of us decisively. Let us ponder these two sides.

In Jesus the human being, we experience God and nothing less. "God was in Christ" (2 Cor. 5:19), the Bible says. Something profoundly important for our praying is at stake here. Jesus does not just give us some knowledge about God so that we are well-informed people; Jesus is the self-giving of God's own self to us. Here God is had by us. God does not escape our grasp, indeed our claim. The event of Jesus, his life, death, and resurrection, is not just something we can talk about but is a constituting event of God's own reality. No longer can one speak of God properly and adequately without speaking of Jesus. Indeed, no longer can one speak of God without also speaking of the world, for in Jesus, God forged an unbreakable link with the world of God's own creation. When we pray in the name of Jesus, we ground our prayer on this link and on nothing else. God is had by us in prayer, for to pray in the name of Jesus is to lay claim to the indissoluble linkage of God with this world. Nothing "in all creation, will be able to separate us from the love of God in Christ Jesus our Lord" (Rom. 8:39). God is "stuck" forever with God's world; and we have a claim upon God. Therefore we pray.

At the same time that we are enabled to lay hold of God, God also lays hold of us: we are had by God. This tells us of God's initiative. That we can lay hold of God rests on the fact that God first lays hold of us. But more is at stake for our understanding of prayer in the name of Jesus than simply that God is the first actor, the grace-giving agent. God, in fact, is more than Jesus. It was, after all, the Father to whom Jesus prayed. In fact, God is more than just the Father and Jesus together: "And I will pray the Father, and he will give you another Counselor, to be with you for ever, even the Spirit of truth" (John 14:16). There we have it: God has us in a threefold way—as the creative transcendence Jesus called Father, as the redeeming occurrence people named Jesus, and as the abiding presence Jesus called the Spirit. Christian prayer, therefore, is not only prayer "in the name of Jesus" but also prayer "in the Spirit." For "no one can say 'Jesus is Lord' except by the Holy Spirit" (1 Cor. 12:3).

The consequence of this for our understanding of prayer is profound. The Spirit is God's power to be with the world as Creator, as Redeemer, and as its final future Consummation. Not only so, it is the Spirit that lies behind, beneath, and within all prayer, even as breath lies before and within life. Indeed the cosmos itself is animated by God's Spirit, such that not only our groans but the groans of creation are the groans of the Spirit (Romans 8). The Spirit is the breath of the universe, a praying breath. And behind this lies a marvel we do not often consider: prayer is proper to God's own being. Traditional theology has fancy terms for that—like "perichoresis" or "circumincession." The Son gives thanks to the Father in the Spirit. God is in perpetual communication, always giving and always receiving. And that has consequence for us, for "he who searches the hearts of men knows what is the mind of the Spirit, because the Spirit intercedes for the saints according to the will of God" (Rom. 8:27). We are thereby invited in the Spirit to become participants in the divine conversation. We become prayer partners with God. In this way, God lays full claim upon our lives.

We have struggled with some difficult questions in this essay. The questions are not easy to answer. The invitation to prayer, according to the Scriptures, is a universal invitation: "Let all that breathes praise the Lord." As we tried to take this seriously, we found that we had partially to rethink our understanding of God and of how the God of Jesus relates to both the God of Israel and the many gods and many lords of the Gentiles. Finally, we found that we were driven back to a Christian understanding of "God in Christ" and of what it means to pray "in Jesus' name." At the end, we realized what a comprehensive claim was set forth in this little phrase, and we discovered that prayer is God's own proper activity, for God is a community and we are graciously made partakers of that communion by the power of the Spirit. And it is this Spirit that breathes the possibility of prayer into the whole of creation. Thus, we conclude as we began: "Let all that breathes praise the Lord."

NOTES

1. Kenneth Cragg, *Alive to God: Muslim and Christian Prayer* (London: Oxford Univ. Press, 1970), 2.

2. "The universal aspect of living revelation is emphasized in the Genesis accounts of creation and the Noachic covenant (chs. 1–9), and is never lost sight of thereafter, though the Bible focuses upon the Abrahamic covenant through the lineage of Jacob (Israel) (Gen. 17). However, the Abrahamic covenant is richly suggestive of a biblical perspective upon Muhammad, whose lineage in the Islamic biographies is traced back through to the descendants of Ishmael. The latter, in Genesis, is placed firmly within God's covenant with Abraham, for which reason he was circumcised (17:26–27), and 17:20 records the divine assurance that 'I shall bless him and make him fruitful and multiply him exceedingly; he shall be father of twelve princes and I will make him a great nation' (cf. Isa. 60:7–8)" (David A. Kerr, "The Prophet Muhammad in Christian Theological Perspective," *International Bulletin* 1984): 116 n. 35.

3. For a further discussion of the call to prayer and of Muslim devotions in general, see Constance E. Padwick, *Muslim Devotions: A Study of Prayer-Manuals in Common Use* (London: SPCK, 1961).

4. Cragg, *Alive to God*, 2–3.

5. The Hebrew and Greek terms for "spirit" (*ruach* in the Old Testament, *pneuma* in the New Testament) mean "breath," "wind."

6. *Rig Veda* 2.12.2 Cited from *The Vedic Experience Mantramanjari: An Anthology of the Vedas for Modern Man and Contemporary Celebration*, ed. and trans. Raimundo Pannikar (Berkeley and Los Angeles: Univ. of California Press, 1977), 202.

7. *Rig Veda* 2.12.10 (*The Vedic Experience Mantramanjari*, 203).

8. *Atharva Veda* 4.16.1 (*Matramanjari*, 512).

9. *Rig Veda* 7.89.5 (*Matramanjari*, 518).

10. *Shih Ching* Mao no. 198 (Ch'ao-yen of the Hsiao-ya). Cited with modifications from David Howard Smith's *Chinese Religions* (New York: Holt, Rinehart & Winston, 1968), 20.

11. *Shih Ching* Mao no. 200 (Hsiang-po of the Hsiao-ya; *Chinese Religions*, 20, modified).

12. *Shu Ching* 5.1.2.3. See in James Legge's *The Chinese Classics* (New York: John Balden, 1987), 3:290.

13. Legge, *Chinese Classics*, 295.

14. Ibid., 290.

15. Ibid., 292. See also C. S. Song, *The Compassionate God* (Maryknoll, N.Y.: Orbis Books, 1982), 146–47 and nn.

16. From a lecture by the Venerable Dr. Nandisvara, Theravadan monk, at the Minnesota Zen Meditation Center. See *MZMC News* 10/4 (Winter 1985): 1.

17. William C. Chittick, ed. and trans., *A Shi'ite Anthology* (Albany: State Univ. of New York Press, 1981), 101.

18. Roy A. Harrisville, *Romans* (Minneapolis: Augsburg Pub. House, 1970), 41.

19. Quoted from F. F. Bruce's *Commentary on the Book of the Acts* (Grand Rapids: Wm. B. Eerdmans, 1956), 359. The section quoted by Paul is italicized.

20. Ibid., 360. The section quoted by Paul is italicized.

21. 1 Cor. 10:19–21. I take "demons" to be a functional term and not substantive. After all, Paul already denied the idols substantiality ("nothing").

22. John 14:13–14; 15:16. This is a distinctively Johannine way of speaking about prayer. "In Jesus name" is not a magical formula, however. See Matt. 7:22–23. We use the phrase in the Johannine sense here.

Seven

PRAYER AND ACTION
Loren E. Halvorson

THE CONNECTION

There are many times that I have acted without prayer and have re-
gretted it. There are other times when I went off to prayer and wondered later if I should not have acted first. There are times when I pray
because I do not know what to do. But there are other times when I
pray because I know only too well what I should do.

What is the relationship between prayer and action? First, I will offer
some introductory comments on the connection between prayer and
action. Second, I will explore how a fundamental cultural change is
forcing many activists (like myself) to rediscover prayer. Third, I will
share some personal convictions about how the growing interest in
spirituality affects the way we view prayer and political action.

Dietrich Bonhoeffer, whose prayers led him to an action that even
his friends considered politically radical, once wrote, "Our being
Christian will consist now in these two things, in praying and doing
justice. . . . All thinking, talking and organizing of Christianity
must be born out of this prayer and this action."[1] Many of us, however, are not as clear about the connection of prayer and action as
Bonhoeffer was. We have observed too long in ourselves and in others the separation of the two: we pray and do nothing, or we rush

into action without prayer. Prayer, then, is readily seen as the opposite of action.

An educational program in Pittsburgh targets high-school drop
outs, mostly black, for tutoring by volunteers. It is a partnership effort
between local congregations and high schools. Retired Roman Catholic sisters who are no longer actively employed have joined in the program. Every day these sisters receive the names of the students and
volunteers involved and pray for them. They can no longer "act"—but
their prayers *are* their action and a very important part of the program
to restore dignity and worth to the students. When I was told about this
connection of prayer and action in Pittsburgh, I realized that the two
must be approached in relation to each other and not in isolation.

The ancient formulation of the connection between prayer and action is *Ora et labora,* "Pray and work." This formula does not tell us to
pray and then work, although the word "pray" does appear first. And
certainly it does not invite the option of praying *or* working. The "and,"
I believe, allows us a certain ambiguity as to how prayer and action are
related. The "and" invites us to wrestle with the relationship. It does
not allow us to separate the two as in "Some pray, others work," "Pray
and you don't have to do everything," "If prayer doesn't work, then do
it yourself," "Prayer is superior to work," "Prayer will tell you what to
do, then do it," "Pray on Sunday and then work the rest of the week,"
"Prayer applies to some things, work applies to other things."

The biblical injunction to "pray without ceasing" may well be the ori-
gin of *Ora et labora.* The point to be stressed in Christian prayer is that
both aspects belong together as inhaling and exhaling do for breathing
and as sleep and activity belong together for life. One is not possible
without the other. Granting the inseparability of the two, I would
nonetheless like to explore what follows from starting with one or the
other. In beginning with one or the other, we will find different consequences, and in examining these differences, we will, I believe, learn
something about prayer.

The phrase *Ora et labora* comes out of the monastic tradition and out
of a culture that placed God at the center of reality. To begin with
prayer, therefore, was a natural consequence of the values of that age.
There was still mystery to many aspects of existence. The Enlightenment had not yet instilled the kind of confidence that could work first

(examining, reasoning, experimenting, exploring) and then turn to God for solace or further guidance. Nor had the despair and cynicism of the contemporary world yet laid its deadening doubts on the human spirit. God was the ultimate reality to which one turned at the outset, not the absent One whose address was unknown.

But at their worst, monastic practices led to the separation of prayer and action. Either there was the superior vocation of prayer, separated from life in a cloister alone with God, or there was the wielding of power by rich religious communities whose work bore little evidence of the disciplines of prayer. The church that prays and then does not act is as unfaithful as the church that acts but forgets prayer.

There have also been moments in the history of the church when prayer has been placed in opposition to human works. I think of the attempt by religious authorities to regulate work, control thought, manage economic and political systems, and even destroy opponents, all because of a superior wisdom claimed on the basis of prayer. This certainly represents a sad and ugly chapter in history. And that is at least one reason that the modern world is often suspicious of those who pray.

Today, especially in the Western world, we are more likely to reverse the sequence: *Labora et ora.* Our pragmatic, God-is-absent-lost-or-indifferent secularism does not hesitate to plunge into activity. Many of us who do pray do so after we work, when we are "at the end of our ropes." We turn in desperation to God to complete what we have not finished ourselves or what we cannot finish ourselves or to lament our failures or to ask God to concur with our conclusions or to bless our already-accomplished endeavors. Prayer has become for many a matter of therapy, a clinical appointment to straighten out the mess we have made; prayer is also seen as a kind of insurance policy, an effort to guarantee and preserve what we have done. Prayer tends to be what we do afterward; but our will, our agenda, comes first. Sunday is seen as the end of the week, not the beginning. God is viewed in a utilitarian way as the enabler of the human enterprise and not vice versa. Religion is given a place in the modern pantheon because it soothes the troubled psyche. In such a view, prayer is clearly not the springboard for action. Prayer may be the ritual at the beginning of the board or committee meeting, but even in the ecclesiastical meeting it is certainly not the main business at hand.

Action must be deeply rooted in spirituality. Action that does not issue from one's deepest roots can easily become activism and may be a way of veiling an empty center like that of Peer Gynt's famous onion after the last layer had been peeled off. As many busy persons can attest, it is hard to live very long with the core missing, with no heart in the matter. I believe it was Gandhi who said that "it is better to put one's heart into one's prayers without finding the right words, than to find the right words without putting one's heart into them." Naturally we want the right words. But words, to be authentic, must have an authentic self behind them. In *Out of Solitude*, Henri Nouwen says,

> Somewhere we know that without silence words lose their meaning, that without listening speaking no longer heals, that without distance closeness cannot cure. Somewhere we know that without a lonely place our actions quickly become empty gestures.[2]

Nouwen is pleading for solitude, that is, time for the primary verb. His model for this is Jesus. Jesus would rise "long before dawn." Nouwen believes that in those special moments we find the secret of Jesus' ministry. Jesus took time for the journey inward. "A luxury," we say defensively, "a nice thing if you had the time." But just imagine this, if you will. Here is this Jewish call committee that has waited thousands of years for the messiah to show up. When he does, he announces that he has only thirty-six months for the assignment and that he wants the first forty days off!

Human history has received more from those who had time off for inward journeys than from those who did not. Again and again it has been the selves emerging from the solitude of the desert, exile, prison, the edge, who have made the significant contributions: Paul, Luther, Julian of Norwich, Bonhoeffer, Sojourner Truth, Gandhi. These persons have all had their prison and exile experiences, where they came to know themselves and God. They have all been active contemplatives—that is, they brought a center to their actions and action out of their centers. Their action has been rooted in solitude, anchored in contemplation.

If someone had told me fifteen years ago, in the midst of busy street activities and of teaching courses on "church and society" that I would end up in the woods in a contemplative, ecumenical retreat community, I would have said, "Impossible." I could not have seen then that the way to be truly present in the street as a caring person was through the solitude of the desert. The ecumenical part I would have understood, but not the contemplative. I had been taught to be suspect of the monastic as irresponsible inaction. Only after the hectic 1960s, the sorting-out of the 1970s, and all the burned-out and dropped-out friends from those days have I discovered the connection between prayer, contemplation, retreat, and healing action.

Christ's time in the desert was certainly not withdrawal from responsible action but the way toward responsible action. His life was literally consumed serving others. The desert was the place where Jesus engaged in the deepest struggle of all. That is where he faced the heart of the matter. The most profoundly private moment was the most public. The actions that followed were determined in that moment apart. In the desert the real self is discovered in the context of God and neighbor. In her book *Journey Outward*, Elizabeth O'Connor says,

> If engagement with ourselves does not push back horizons so that we see neighbors we did not see before, then we need to examine the appointment kept with self. If prayer does not drive us into some concrete involvement at a point of the world's need, then we must question prayer; . . . the inner life is not nurtured in order to hug to oneself some secret gain.[3]

This, I believe, is what the term *meditatio* should mean, and at times did mean in the Cistercian monastaries in Scotland and Ireland in the tenth and eleventh centuries. The cloistered years of inner discipline might easily appear socially irrelevent from the outside, but they were actually preparation for concrete action. That time was the prelude for lives of intensive service bringing the gospel to pagan Europe. The hardships of poor food, modest clothing, limited shelter, and unfriendly natives were so severe that the monks lived to the average age of twenty-four! Their time in preparation was not passive. "To be" is an active verb. Monastic *meditatio* is like the split second before the gun goes off in the hundred-yard dash. The runner appears to be passive but really is not. Everything within is poised, ready. The race has already begun within.

Properly understood, prayer is a subversive activity.[4] The desert fathers and mothers were the radicals of their time, for they removed themselves from the traditional social roles in protest against the values of their culture. They were often consulted by those seeking an alternative course of action. The inward journey is a dangerous one, for it leads to basic changes in the direction of one's whole life. In this sense the private is most public. The most significant role—indeed, the unique role—of the church in society is to provide a journey so deeply inward that the whole of life is transformed.

The social paralysis that prevails in an age of confusion results in no small part, I believe, from the absence of a framework of meaning, that is, from the absence of a solid basis for action. The journey inward reveals the connectedness of faith and action. I would argue further that if God's people are not actively engaged in the world it may be because they are not radically disengaged from the world. The religious activities of worship, personal faith, mission, evangelism, and the like, can become tamed, domesticated, and boxed in, and may then no longer challenge private or public agendas. To maintain that social action starts with prayer may surprise many, but not those who have been deeply involved in such action and recognize how essential deep roots are for sustained action. Nor will it surprise those who have been deeply engaged in prayer and know the claims God makes on one's whole life.

When I was in China some years ago, the government was beginning to open many closed congregations. I wondered at the time if the public authorities were less afraid of visible and regularized religious practices than of what goes on in the secret, mysterious life of the church underground. Bonhoeffer touched on this in his fascination with the "secret disciplines" of Christians living under persecution in the early church. Bonhoeffer's own underground activities revealed to him the power, and threat, of the inward journey, and he even suggested that the church would have more impact on society if it made its public worship more private and its personal discipleship more public.

IMPASSE AND CHANGE

Whoever is unwilling to pray should beware of action. Whoever is unwilling to act should beware of prayer. It has taken me many years to appreciate this caution.[5] I am one who had been wary or impatient with prayer because I had not understood how it related to action. Too many prayers appeared to me unconcerned with, or even opposed to, action. At best they meant a dependency on God's action that lifted

the human actor off the hook. After some decades of attempting to ac-
tivate God's people in society and after becoming more aware of the
motives and character of my own action, I find myself less confident
about initiating action apart from prayer. An account of how I came to
this point will assist the reader in understanding my overall argument.

There is one moment that stands out as pivotal in my coming to view
prayer with a renewed and urgent interest. It occurred in the late 1960s
after the publication of the Kerner Report, which graphically docu-
mented the upheavals in American cities in the summers of 1967 and
1968. John Gardner, then head of the National Urban Coalition, summoned a representative group of leaders from American life—
business, education, media, government—to his offices in Washington, D.C., to discuss the report and to share ideas about what might be
done in various sectors of American society to redress the problems of
racism. A Catholic friend with whom I had worked to organize community dialogues in Detroit after the riots was invited, along with me,
to represent the religious community.

During the consultation, a recurring theme of the Kerner Report
was raised, namely, the recognition that a fundamental change in the
heart and soul of white American was needed. That agenda, however, no group felt competent to undertake. Finally the others turned
to the two of us from the church and said, "Who's supposed to do
that? The Post Office Department?" What remains in my memory
from that day is the surprise to someone like me, who was trying to
learn as much as I could of action in society, to be reminded by people
speaking from a secular perspective that they saw the churches' most
significant social role as the conversion of the "heart, mind, and soul
of America." That laid the seeds for a process within me that began to
bear fruit a decade later.

I began my academic career in physics interested to know what is really "out there," what can be measured, felt, shaped, managed, im-
proved. And to my surprise it was a paleontologist (Chardin) and a
physicist (Capra) who persuaded me (long after formal theological
study) that there is no "thing" out there, no elemental particle at the
center of the material world, but movement and spirit! The key to
human knowledge is, in the last analysis, not empirical inquiry but
something deeper. An old friend from the urban activism of the 1960s
has stated the paradox more eloquently than I could:

Objectivism, by reducing the world to a collection of things, places the
knower in a field of mute and inert objects that passively succumb to his
or her definitions of them. In this sense, objectivism creates the most
subjective of worlds, a world created in our own images, a world of objects that cannot fight back and assert their own selfhood. . . . In prayer
we acknowledge the spiritual bonds that tie us and our world together.
Prayer is the way of paradox—a way of entering into silence so deeply
that we can hear the whole world's speech, a way of entering into solitude so deeply that we can fill the whole world's connections. In prayer
we touch that transcendent Spirit from whom all things arise and to
whom all things return, who makes all things kindred as they go.[6]

I have undertaken the writing of this chapter with some hesitation.
Though I have taught for many years in a theological seminary, I am
very much in need of instruction in prayer. I am not alone, for I believe that our lack of wisdom and experience regarding prayer has to
do with the beginning of a basic shift in the way we in Western culture think—a kind of epistemological revolution. There is a change
from the studied effort to know, to the vulnerability of being known;
from the effort of will and intellect, to listening to heart and intuition;
from left brain, to right brain; from determining, deciding, planning,
controlling beforehand, to risking the uncontrolled, awaiting the un-
expected, and receiving the One who comes in mystery; from talking
and writing about prayer, to practicing, and acting out of, the discipline of prayer.

This cultural revolution suggests a shift in one's mode of being and
doing that so radically reverses, upsets, and disorients that it
amounts to a conversion or a passage through Alice's mirror. In it the
same reality is seen, the same data observed, but everything is different, perhaps even opposite, and new conclusions and actions result.
The radical reversal in direction is so traumatic that elaborate
schemes are often spawned to avoid the exodus from the familiar and
predictable. The revolution is one of perception, of spirituality. In one
sense nothing changes, in another sense everything changes. Although the empirical and the experiential are part of the data re-
viewed with new eyes, I believe that the change has more to do with
vision than analysis, serendipity than calculation, the Holy Spirit
than prescribed ritual or dogma.

The turning point warrants the label of impasse. An impasse is a
point where no further progress is possible by simply increasing the

same efforts. An entirely new direction must be taken before one can return and move ahead:

> The psychologist and the theologian, the poet and the mystic, assure us that impasse can be the condition for creative growth and transformation *if* the experience of impasse is fully appropriated within one's heart and flesh with consciousness and consent; *if* the limitations of one's humanity and human condition are squarely faced and the sorrow of finitude allowed to invade the human spirit with real, existential powerlessness; *if* the ego does not demand understanding in the name of control and predictability but is willing to admit the mystery of its own being and surrender itself to this mystery; *if* the path into the unknown, into the uncontrolled and unpredictable margins of life, is freely taken when the path of deadly clarity fades.[7]

The exercise of breathing is an excellent illustration of this point. If you choose only to inhale, the moment will soon come when survival drives one to exhale. It is a matter of life and death. In inhaling and exhaling, to do one to the exclusion of the other leads to excessive expressions in the opposite direction, to a kind of unnatural breathing, far too conscious of itself, too violent, too studied, too artificial, too exaggerated, too reactionary. The more natural and healthy state would be the unforced practice (*habitus*) of doing both in balanced sequence. If indeed, as I believe, the movement of many today toward prayer and spirituality comes out of impasse, we need to be alert to the dangers as well as the necessity of moving in new directions not only for one moment but as an ongoing practice: "Pray without ceasing," implies "Pray and act without ceasing" just as "Breathe without ceasing" implies "Inhale and exhale without ceasing." Inhaling may appear to be the opposite of exhaling but organically it is not. Quite the contrary, inhaling and exhaling are interdependent as the primal exercise of life itself.

I believe that our culture is at an impasse where further development in nearly every area (economics, education, policy formation, health care, intellectual growth, community development, artistic expression, spirituality) will be impossible until we voluntarily dare or involuntarily are driven to move in the opposite direction. As in breathing, a reversal sustains life. What does this suggest about our approach to prayer? I believe that we need to see prayer in the context of our larger cultural crisis, or impasse. Our problem with prayer is not with prayer itself; that is, it is not with just one part of the modern

human experience which as an isolated datum needs only to be ex-
humed, examined, explained and demystified in the light of science
and reason. The issue is fundamental because it brings us to the center
of reality whose further self-disclosure will not yield to our academic
pursuit—no matter how brilliant—until a radically different approach
is undertaken.

Is it possible that in our time the elite of the world are being invited
by God into darkness rather than enlightenment, into ignorance rather
than knowledge, into silence rather than speech, into being questioned
rather than providing answers, into childhood rather than adulthood,
into being formed again like a mute and helpless embryo in the womb
of reality rather than remaining secure professionals? Unlearning
("unknowing," in the language of the mystics) is far more difficult than
initial learning. What is involved here is not just the curious mind's
being satisfied but the willful pride's being challenged. The shift from
knowledge to wisdom is a radical but not an alien one.

A new Reformation may not be born out of prayer nor because of
prayer nor even because of the absence of prayer, but it may be born
out of the impasse with prayer. "Not knowing" is a good place to begin,
though some of us may be so addicted to trying to know that we need a
twelve-step recovery program of which the first step is to admit one's
helplessness. One is always a beginner when it comes to prayer. Therefore it is not surprising that there is much tentativeness in our writing
and speaking about prayer. We are apt to use the poetic language of vision more than the prose of analytical analysis. But such writing may
inspire even when it fails to instruct.

BEING PRESENT TO THE WORLD

Finally, I would like to explore how action rooted in prayer can impact public life. In short, I want to ask what the relationship is between
prayer and political action. In recent years I have begun to appreciate
how the church can become present to the world through prayer itself.
I have begun to rediscover the monastic tradition, in which the apparent withdrawal from the world to learn the spiritual disciplines of
meditatio is actually a means of readying oneself for being fully present
to the world. (As I have mentioned, the Cistercians of the tenth and
eleventh centuries afford a particularly strong example of this.) The

monastic tradition has drawn Christians deeply into the lives and affairs of people.

We need to be absent in order to be present, to withdraw in order to draw near, to leave in order to enter. Prayer appears to be an escape from the public into the personal and private. But, as John Macquarrie has noted, there is no such thing as private prayer: it is always a communal activity. Prayer is the way we enter most deeply into the human, social, political realities. As Bonhoeffer was drawn more deeply into prayer, he was drawn more deeply into political action and vice versa. I for one believe that the Bonhoeffer of *Life Together* (the meditator in monastic retreat) and the Bonhoeffer of *Letters from Prison* (the political actor) are the same person. Matthew Fox calls prayer a "radical response to life" and Charles Elliot, the economist and theologian, concludes his book on global economics and the church with the comment that our best hope appears to be small groups of Christians "going inward in radical contemplation and outward in radical action."[8] You cannot have one without the other.

> The truth is that prayer and action, the inward and the outward, are bound together in such a close reciprocity that it makes no sense to ask which comes first. They are in constant interaction. Prayer interprets the world, and the world interprets prayer.[9]

Perhaps the impasse in our political engagement is actually the impasse in our prayer life and we need to turn from one to the other in order to break through the impasse. I once had an interesting conversation with a Methodist bishop about the impasse he encountered with several committees. With a twinkle in his eye he declared, "I think I will assign social action to the evangelism committee and evangelism to the social action committee." The function of impasse, of coming to the limits, is to turn us around to recover essential ingredients that have been lost or devalued.

Struggle with impasse exposes the deeper motives, it reveals the stranger within, it burrows beyond the how to the why, it exposes the root system. To reach that level where one surrenders one's will and admits one's limitation ("Pray as if everything depends on God") paradoxically brings a new freedom to act (" . . . and work as if everything depends on you"). Prayer unites control (surrendering to God's will in faith) and freedom ("Love and do as you please"). This paradox arises from the nature of prayer as a discipline that liberates. Arthur Schnabel, the Austrian pianist, says about interpreting musical scores, "When you know the why, you can improvise." Prayer is not convincing God of the rightness of my cause but becoming in tune with God's cause: "Not my will but thy will." And when we remain unclear or even when we have decided on a course of action, the defeat of our efforts is not disastrous. It is not our task to shape reality nor control the course of history but to root our action in God's action. And that means action that is compassionate and concrete. The point has been made in this way:

> If the emphasis on prayer were an escape from direct engagement with the many needs and pains of our world, then it would not be a real discipline of the compassionate life. Prayer challenges us to be fully aware of the world in which we live and to present it with all its needs and pains to God. It is this compassionate prayer that calls for compassionate action. . . . Prayer without action grows into powerless pietism, and action without prayer degenerates into questionable manipulation. If prayer leads us into a deeper unity with the compassionate Christ, it will always give rise to concrete acts of service. . . . In prayer we meet Christ, and in him all human suffering. In service we meet people, and in them the suffering Christ.[10]

Prayer that precedes action is not flight from involvement but the mining through contemplation and meditation of the soil on which one lives. Monastic withdrawal is not to some safe place of escape but to the threshold of action, that is, the threshold of God's action. This point has been made recently by Parker Palmer in an article suggesting that monasticism is the way for church renewal:

> At the heart of the monastic experiment is a simple premise, naive to some and self evident to others, yet radical in its implications: *God is alive, well, and at work in us and in our world.* . . . Many of us and our congregations are guilty of "functional atheism." Though our language pays lip service to God, our actions assume that God does not exist or is in a coma. *Functional atheism is the belief that nothing is happening unless we make it happen.* It is the belief behind our unwillingness to take silence and solitude seriously.[11]

Thomas Merton's withdrawal to a Trappist monastery was not escape from action but a way of moving more deeply into the world of action. It was while in the monastery that Merton exposed deeply the realities of Auschwitz, Hiroshima, and Selma. Merton's words spoke powerfully to people at the barricades in the 1960s. Prayer invites us on a more difficult journey than mere action. In prayer we decide not on our strategy, what we should do in a given situation, but on what God is doing. Prayer may interfere or remove us from our own agendas, but it takes us to the threshold of God's action. Dag Hammarskjold, a person of considerable involvement, called this journey the longest and hardest of all. He wrote, "The road to holiness necessarily passes through the world of action."[12]

Surely a hopeful sign for the prayer life of the church today is the emergence of a spirituality that is searching for earthy values again: in materiality (Chardin, Capra), in politics (liberation theology), among the poor (the base-community movement), and in the major movements of our time (feminism, ecology, global justice).[13] This spiritual search is like an archaeological dig into the past and present that can yield a new vision for the future. The deeper we penetrate mystery, the deeper our political action can become; and the deeper the engagement in political struggle, the deeper the sense of mystery can grow. To be most fully present to one's own reality, however, requires a trust that is increasingly rare in a society filled with lawyers and litigation as well as nuclear weapons. An age that trusts only what it can explain or control has lost the sense of mystery and seeks knowledge and power frenetically.

As humans face one another with increasing suspicion and fear and enter one another's orbits armed with awesome and complicated weapons that technology cannot by itself control, prayer becomes neither a luxury nor a pious escape but a necessary and highly practical course. For now we all need to ask, "Lord, teach us to pray." The connection between prayer and action has to do with the survival of all of life. Survival depends on trust. That trust is based not on a liberal optimism but on the deeper truth that as we "seek the shalom" of the other we will find our own shalom (Jer. 29:4–7). Trust cannot be based on being number one. Such arrogance is as disastrous for others as it is for ourselves, for it creates the very conditions that guarantee the destruction of the world. Prayer is the discipline on the way to action that relinquishes control and seeks direction from another. Prayer is not the last and hopeless act when all else has failed but the preparatory one for healing action. Rooted in prayer, our actions need not be fearful, strident, or manipulative, but they must be peacemaking. So we return to the place where we began: "Our being Christian will consist now in these two things, in praying and doing justice."

NOTES

1. Thomas Day, *Dietrich Bonhoeffer on Christian Community and Common Sense* (Lewiston, N.Y.: Edwin Mellen Press, 1983), 212.
2. Henri Nouwen, *Out of Solitude* (Notre Dame, Ind.: Ave Maria Press, 1974), 14.
3. Elizabeth O'Connor, *Journey Inward, Journey Outward* (New York: Harper & Row, 1968).
4. Cf. Michael Cosby, *Thy Will Be Done: Praying the Our Father as Subversive Activity* (Maryknoll, N.Y.: Orbis Books, 1977).
5. This formulation is taken, with some adaptations, from Dietrich Bonhoeffer's *Life Together*: "Whoever cannot be alone should be aware of community and whoever cannot be in community should beware of being alone."
6. Parker Palmer, *To Know As We Are Known* (New York: Harper & Row, 1983), 56, 124.
7. Constance Fitzgerald, "Impasse and Dark Night," in *Living with Apocalypse*, ed. T. H. Edwards (San Francisco: Harper & Row, 1984), 96.
8. See Matthew Fox, *On Becoming a Musical, Mystical Bear: Spirituality American-Style* (New York: Harper & Row, 1972), chap. 3; and Charles Elliot, *Inflation and the Compromised Church* (Belfast: Christian Journals, 1975), 145.
9. John Macquarrie, *Paths in Spirituality* (London: SCM Press, 1972), 20–21.
10. Donald P. McNeill, Douglas Morrison, and Henri Nouwen, *Compassion* (Garden City, N.Y.: Doubleday & Co., 1983), 116–17.
11. Parker Palmer, "The Monastic Way to Church Renewal," *Salt and Light* (March 1986).
12. Dag Hammarskjold, *Markings* (London: Faber & Faber, 1964), 108. Cf. Charles Peguy, *Temporal and Eternal* (London: Harvill Press, 1958), 45: "Originally, primitively, the mystical life, the Christian operation amounted to and consisted, not in avoiding the world, but in saving the world, not in hiding from it, but, *on the contrary*, consisted of nourishing the world mystically."
13. This point is aptly made by Alan Ecclestone, *A Staircase for Silence* (London: Darton, Longman & Todd, 1977), 50: "Our concern for the world was often too shallow to make it a matter of spiritual choice at all. We proposed to abstain from what we had never known. The result was clear. Our spirituality has been to a disastrous extent precociously metaphysical. We have lacked the sap of the earth to give life to our dealings with Heaven. . . . Our praying too often and to too large an extent lacks earth to nourish it."

PART THREE

THE PRACTICE
OF PRAYER

Eight

THE KINGDOM PRAYER
David L. Tiede

Our Father in heaven,
hallowed be your name.
Your kingdom come,
your will be done, on earth as in heaven.
Give us today our daily bread.
Forgive us our sins
as we forgive those who sin against us.
Save us from the time of trial
and deliver us from evil.
For the kingdom, the power, and the glory
are yours, now and forever.
Amen.

LORD, TEACH US TO PRAY!

It is the classic Christian prayer, the Lord's Prayer, the Our Father. It is the prayer Jesus taught his disciples, and it has been taught to every generation, to millions of Christians, in thousands of languages for hundreds of years. It is the standard for all Christian prayer, constantly offered throughout the world at baptisms and burials, for family meals and the Lord's Supper, in thanksgiving and through tears. It is the prayer of the one who is Messiah and Lord and Son of God, revealing

107

the reign of God to all the mortal race. Its fabric of comfort is woven with the human heritage of its long usage, and its call to God for the coming of the kingdom is a prophetic witness to the mercy and justice of the dominion of Jesus in the present time.

Historically, the prayer is remarkable for its similarity to other prayers of the first century. The authoritarian and antiquated "kingdom" language and the patriarchal address of God as Father are strange and offensive to many people in the modern era, but these were standard features of Jesus' world. Furthermore, Jesus' distinctive understanding of the hope of God's gracious reign may be better grasped when compared with other concepts of God's dominion. Those who declare all such language of power or patriarchy to be simply unacceptable may only silence the powerless once again. But when are these terms liberating and saving and when are they repressive and enslaving?

In the New Testament period, God "our Father, our King" was so consistently addressed in royal terms that one rabbi said that "a prayer in which there is no mention of kingship is no prayer."[1] The Pharisaic and early rabbinic traditions that survived beyond the first century were filled with similar praise and prayers to the God who rules heaven and earth. A few illustrations must suffice.

From the Shema and its benedictions:

> You are praised, O Lord our God
> Sovereign of the universe,
> Fashioner of light and Creator of darkness,
> Maker of peace and Creator of all.
> In mercy You give light to the earth
> and to those who dwell upon it.
>
> Praised be His Name,
> whose glorious kingdom is forever and ever.
>
> May our eyes see,
> our hearts rejoice,
> and our souls truly be glad
> in your salvation,
> when Zion will be told:
> "Your God is enthroned!"
> The Lord rules;
> The Lord has ruled;
> The Lord shall rule forever and ever.

> For yours is the kingdom,
> and unto all eternity You will reign in glory;
> for beside You we have no King.[2]

From the opening stanza of the kaddish prayer:

> Exalted and hallowed be His great Name
> in the world which He created
> according to his will.
> May He establish His kingdom
>   [Some rites add:
>   and cause His salvation to sprout,
>   and hasten the coming of His messiah,]
> in your lifetime and in your days,
> and in the lifetime of the whole
> household of Israel
> speedily and at a near time.
> And say: Amen.[3]

Of course people had been praying long before Jesus and his Jewish contemporaries. Some of those prayers also displayed a profound sense of divine dominion throughout human affairs. The prayers of the Stoic philosopher Cleanthes (331–233 B.C.) are striking examples of the clarity of pre-Christian Greek theology. The first stanza of his "Hymn to Zeus," for example, reveals the Stoic sense of divine sovereignty as exercised in natural law:

> Most glorious of immortals, Zeus
> The many-named, almighty evermore,
> Nature's great Sovereign, ruling all by law—
> Hail to thee! On thee 'tis meet and right
> That mortals everywhere should call.
> From thee was our begetting; ours alone
> Of all that live and move upon the earth
> The lot to bear god's likeness.
> Thee will I ever chant, thy power praise.[4]

Many interesting comparisons may be made between Jesus' prayer for the kingdom and the prayers of his contemporaries. Certainly the dynamic character of the God to whom Jesus prays stands out in contrast to the impersonal and fatalistic theology of the Stoics. The kingdom for which Jesus prays may even subvert the apparent authority of the hierarchical "powers that be," with its forgiveness and concern for daily bread; and this reign will challenge all claims to "divine right" or ultimate authority by the principalities and governments of this world.

But the prayer itself is neither argumentative nor sectarian. Its contents are not even exclusively Christian[5]—which ought not be surprising when the pre-Easter origins of the prayer are remembered. Furthermore, many non-Christian religious traditions have surprised Christians by their admiration for and use of it. Jesus' prayer for the kingdom of God is deeply grounded in human yearning for divine justice and mercy, and it has proved able to transcend vast cultural differences and to give voice to the hopes of all kinds of people to keep body and soul together within God's purposes and order.

Did Jesus himself have a sharper agenda in mind?[6] It seems unlikely that Jesus was interested only in general spiritual verities. Matthew's Gospel says that Jesus taught this prayer to his disciples in the midst of the critique of those who "practice their piety before others" and the "hypocrites" who "love to stand and pray in the synagogues and at the street corners" in order to be seen by others, and the Gentiles who "heap up empty phrases . . . for they think they will be heard for their many words" (6:1–9). Luke suggests that it was while Jesus himself was praying that one of his disciples requested, "Lord, teach us to pray, as John taught his disciples"; and then Jesus introduced the prayer. In both cases, the practices of others beyond Jesus' circle of followers provided the context. No criticism of John is implied in Luke (see Luke 7:26–28). The criticism of the "hypocrites" and Gentiles in Matthew's text is not directly part of the prayer itself, but because these people play to the human gallery when they pray, the modesty of Jesus' prayer stands out in Matthew's version in contrast to such displays. God is the audience for true prayer, and God does not need extensive instruction.

Luke's briefer version of the prayer is probably closer to Jesus' actual words, and Jesus is even less interested in scoring fine points with his human hearers by means of the prayer. If his kingdom prayer sounds a great deal like other Jewish or Gentile prayers, only simpler, so be it. The glorification of God, the call for God's reign, and the petitions for daily bread, forgiveness, and preservation from trial are all fundamental to human trust in God. The prayer's elegant simplicity of confidence in God is much more distinctive than its originality.

On the other hand, it would be very foolish to forget that Jesus' own vision of his mission in God's reign glistens through all of the Gospel accounts. His prayer for the coming of the kingdom could never have been banal, and his words in this prayer certainly had particular meanings for his disciples who had heard him announce the kingdom. But in the prayer, Jesus was not instructing his disciples or God. He was addressing God and inviting his followers to join an immense human community, gathering up the hopes, fears, and visions of those who trust in the promises of the God of the Scriptures of Israel.

GOD HAS MADE THIS JESUS WHOM YOU CRUCIFIED LORD AND MESSIAH!

The New Testament declares not only that Jesus Christ taught the kingdom prayer but that he is God's answer to the prayer as the Messiah and Lord of God's dominion on earth. The broad human hopes for divine justice and mercy have been acknowledged and gathered in Jesus' prayer, and now God has vindicated him. His prayer for the kingdom has been validated as the agenda of God's reign in the world. Jesus is not merely a spiritual guide with a profound wisdom. In fact, efforts to illumine his spiritual insight may be misguided if the "religion of Jesus" is simply equated with the Christian faith. The Christian faith is decisively post-Easter. Everything that came before is seen in a new light, including Jesus' apparent failure to inaugurate the reign of God by cleansing the temple.[7]

The language on this side of Easter is also "royal" and "theocratic." When the New Testament speaks of Jesus as Christ and Son of God and Lord and Savior, this is testimony about how Jesus is God's way or agent for exercising dominion in the world. Christians proclaimed this post-Easter gospel for some years before any of our New Testament books were written. Thus when Paul cites traditional hymns concerning Jesus as Son of God (Rom. 1:3b–4) or as the Christ (Messiah) who was "in the form of God" (Phil. 2:6–11), he is presenting the crucified Jesus as the ruler whose dominion as a servant God has vindicated and exalted in resurrection. But this proclamation was not original with Paul, nor did it end with him.

The canonical Gospels are also primarily Christian interpretations of the Jesus story, proclaiming God's reign in and through Jesus the Messiah. They are all narrated in the retrospect of Easter, and the historical reminiscence they contain is rallied to clarify, enhance, and specify the "good news" they announce. None of the gospels is naive in suggesting that since Good Friday and Easter all human yearnings for divine justice and mercy have simply been satisfied. But all four accounts of the Jesus story are full of the confidence that God has already begun to answer Jesus' prayer for the kingdom in the person and dominion of the Messiah Jesus himself.

The canonical evangelists, therefore, are our instructors in understanding the kingdom prayer as a Christian prayer. As those who have preserved the memories of the words and works of Jesus, they have indirectly equipped us for appreciating the pre-Easter significance of the prayer. But their purpose is to remember the words, deeds, and prayers of the historical Jesus in the light of Jesus' execution, resurrection, and exaltation. It would be foolish to speculate on what might be the meaning or validity of Jesus' kingdom prayer if his story had turned out differently. Even second-guessing the evangelists on what Jesus himself might have had in mind is illegitimate, given the purposes of the narratives. The Jesus of the Gospels is the vindicated Messiah of God's rule on earth and in heaven, and the kingdom for which his disciples now pray is the kingdom of God which Jesus the Messiah inaugurated. Thus his prayers are disclosures of God's will and reign, and they provide indications of the content and mode of appropriate Christian petitions.

Matthew 6:1–18 is an extended discourse by Jesus on prayer and fasting, standing in the middle of Jesus' Sermon on the Mountain in Matthew 5—7. These eighteen verses contain a variety of sayings of Jesus that the evangelist has now collected. In the larger context, Matthew portrays Jesus as the authoritative teacher who defines and declares the "righteousness" of the kingdom. The evangelist repeatedly alerts the reader to the tensions with other authoritative teachers in Israel, namely, the scribes and Pharisees; but for Christian readers (followers of this Messiah), there is never any doubt that "all authority in heaven and on earth has been given" to Jesus (Matt. 28:18). The kingdom prayer stands in the middle of this middle section of Jesus' sermon:

Beware of practicing your piety before people in order to be seen by them; for then you will have no reward from your Father who is in heaven.

Thus, when you give alms, sound no trumpet before you, as the hypocrites do in the synagogues and in the streets, that they may be praised by people. Truly, I say to you, they have their reward. But when you give alms, do not let your left hand know what your right hand is doing, so that your alms may be in secret; and your Father who sees in secret will reward you.

And when you pray, you must not be like the hypocrites; for they love to stand and pray in the synagogues and at the street corners, that they may be seen by people. Truly, I say to you, they have their reward. But when you pray, go into your room and shut the door and pray to your Father who is in secret; and your Father who sees in secret will reward you.

And in praying do not heap up empty phrases as the Gentiles do; for they think that they will be heard for their many words. Do not be like them, for your Father knows what you need before you ask him. Pray then like this:
Our Father who art in heaven,
Hallowed be thy name.
Thy kingdom come.
Thy will be done,
 On earth as it is in heaven.
Give us this day our daily bread,
And forgive us our debts,
 As we also have forgiven our debtors;
And lead us not into temptation,
 But deliver us from evil
For if you forgive people their trespasses, your heavenly Father also will forgive you; but if you do not forgive people their trespasses, neither will your Father forgive your trespasses.

And when you fast, do not look dismal, like the hypocrites, for they disfigure their faces that their fasting may be seen by people. Truly, I say to you, they have their reward. But when you fast, anoint your head and wash your face, that your fasting may not be seen by people but by your Father who is in secret; and your Father who sees in secret will reward you. (Matt. 6:1–18; *anthropoi* is translated as "people")

Matthew's presentation of the prayer bears many marks of the evangelist's interpretation. The criticism against displays of piety runs throughout the whole section with the consistent assurance that the Father "who sees in secret will reward you" (vv. 4, 6, 18). Jesus' prayer is a display of restraint and confidence that God is truly listening and that playing to the human gallery may have its immediate rewards but that it is hypocrisy before God. Verses 14–15 are clearly a further commentary on the difficult issue of how human forgiveness is bound up with God's forgiveness, and Matthew's version states the matter in surprisingly conditional terms.

One of the most interesting features of Matthew's version, however, is the elaboration of the connection or distance between heaven and earth. This is a consistent issue in Matthew's Gospel, in part because Matthew observes the traditional Jewish aversion to using the word "God" and speaks rather of the "kingdom of heaven." In some passages it seems quite clear that the evangelist is speaking exclusively about a future and otherworldly realm, yet Matthew is regularly insistent that Jesus is Lord and Messiah with authority over "heaven and earth." Matthew presents the Father as being "in heaven" (see vv. 9, 14). Yet only Matthew also presents Jesus as praying that God's will be done "on earth as it is in heaven."

Even heavenly-minded Matthew insists that the kingdom prayer is focused upon earth. Heaven is not a contested territory. God rules heaven, and Jesus will be established as God's Lord in heaven without anyone's needing to pray that God's will be done in heaven. But the prayer for the coming of the kingdom and the accomplishment of the will of God must be spoken upon earth. The earth is the realm that is contested, into which God's reign must be petitioned. Thus in presenting the prayer that Jesus taught to the Christian community reading this Gospel, Matthew is fulfilling the commission of the exalted Lord to teach "them to observe all that I have commanded you" (28:20). But now the heavenly and earthly authority of this exalted Jesus has been established among the faithful "to the close of the age." The kingdom prayer is now the authorized Christian prayer, invoking the reign of the Messiah and Lord Jesus and his kingdom to come on earth.

The elegant simplicity of the prayer, therefore, should not lull people into regarding it as merely innocuous or lovely. Mindless repetitions of this prayer may verge on blasphemy, inviting divine judgment, since the invocation of the kingdom of God is neither a mantra nor a benediction on the status quo. Once the kingdom prayer has become a Christian prayer, offered in the wake of the death and resurrection of the Messiah, it is clear that the power of injustice, violence, and repression has been confronted and the ultimacy of the gracious and merciful dominion of Jesus has been vindicated by God.

Luke 11:1–13 is another extended discourse on prayer, once again assembled by an evangelist from several smaller traditional stories. The first two verses appear to have been composed by the evangelist to introduce the prayer itself. Luke frequently alerts the reader to Jesus' practice of prayer, and the comparison with the disciples of John is consistent with other aspects of Luke's narrative. The prayer itself is closely paralleled in Matthew, but Luke appears to have offered fewer additions to the tradition. Verses 5–8 follow the prayer with a story that only Luke tells, and vv. 9–13 complete the discourse with further teachings on prayer (see also Matt. 7:7–11):

> He was praying in a certain place, and when he ceased, one of his disciples said to him, "Lord teach us to pray, as John taught his disciples." And he said to them, "When you pray, say:
> 'Father,
> hallowed be thy name.
> Thy kingdom come.
> Give us each day our daily bread;
> and forgive us our sins
> for we ourselves forgive everyone
> who is indebted to us;
> and lead us not into temptation.'"
> And he said to them, "Which of you who has a friend will go to him at midnight and say to him, 'Friend, lend me three loaves; for a friend of mine has arrived on a journey, and I have nothing to set before him'; and he will answer from within, 'Do not bother me; the door is now shut, and my children are with me in bed; I cannot get up and give you anything'? I tell you, though he will not get up and give him anything because he is his friend, yet because of his importunity he will rise and give him whatever he needs. And I tell you, Ask, and it will be given you; seek, and you will find; knock, and it will be opened to you. For everyone who asks receives, and he who seeks finds, and to him who knocks it will be opened. What father among you, if his son asks for a fish, will instead of a fish give him a serpent; or if he asks for an egg, will give him a scorpion? If you then, who are evil, know how to give good gifts to your children, how much more will the heavenly Father give the Holy Spirit to those who ask him!" (Luke 11:1–13)

Luke sets this discourse on prayer early in the context of Jesus' journey toward Jerusalem, which moves from 9:51 ("He set his face to go to Jerusalem") to 19:41 ("And when he drew near and saw the city he wept over it"). These ten chapters expand Mark's outline with numerous teachings on discipleship, as the reader follows the way of the Lord to its climax in Jerusalem. On the way, Jesus equips the apostles and the seventy for the mission of the kingdom. No suggestion is given that the journey will be easy.[8] When the kingdom of this Messiah advances against the dominion of Satan, Jesus rejoices "in the Holy Spirit" (Luke 10:17–22). And after this discourse on prayer, Jesus is accused of casting out demons by the Beelzebul, the prince of demons, to which accusation he says, "But if it is by the finger of God that I cast out demons, then the kingdom of God has come upon you" (Luke 11:20; see also v. 18, "And if Satan is divided against himself, how will his kingdom stand?"). It is in the midst of this apocalyptic conflict of spirits and dominions that the Jesus of Luke's Gospel teaches his disciples the kingdom prayer.

Luke's message to his own Christian community stands out when the larger plan of his narrative is noticed. This journey motif is a literary convention that had already been employed to tell such epic stories as Homer's *Odyssey* and Israel's journey in the wilderness. The motif of the journey invites the reader to join the pilgrimage, to identify with the struggles, and to relate them to new experiences and contexts. In Luke 11, Jesus' instruction on prayer is offered to people on the way, in the midst of their struggles with the principalities of evil.

Yet neither the face of evil nor the kingdom is simply symbolic or otherworldly in Luke's narrative. Once again the present time (Luke 12:56) is the crucial arena. The reign of God is coming upon Israel in the person of the Messiah Jesus (see Luke 10:9, 11; 11:20; 16:16; 17:20; 19:28).[9] The human characters are caught up in a drama that often seems far beyond them. Satan desires to "sift like wheat" the very apostles whom Jesus has appointed to "eat and drink at my table in my kingdom, and sit on thrones judging the twelve tribes of Israel" (Luke 22:30–31). But the program to which the Spirit has anointed this Messiah Jesus is primarily focused on this earth: "good news to the poor . . . release to the captives . . . recovering of sight to the blind . . . liberty for the oppressed . . . the year of the Lord's jubilee" (Luke 4:18–19). The stories surrounding the prayer for the kingdom demonstrate that this program is thoroughly earthly and liberating for people. Both this substance of Jesus' dominion and his nondominating authority as servant of God will soon be rejected in his execution "at the hands of lawless people" (Acts 2:23). The kingdom for which Jesus prays is revealed in the messianic mission for which he dies.

The kingdom for which Jesus instructs his disciples to pray is not one more oppressive theocracy, where the poor, the marginalized, the aliens, the women and the children are simply "put in their place." This reign is founded in an authority that only God could equip and legitimate from below, in apparent weakness and foolishness. It is a dominion that challenges the legitimacy of usual human systems of power, value, class, and influence. It is a sovereignty of service and forgiveness, committed to life and bread and salvation for those who have need while offering repentance unto forgiveness even to the oppressor: "The kings of the Gentiles exercise lordship over them. . . . But not so with you; rather let the greatest among you become as the youngest, and the leader as one who serves. . . . I am among you as one who serves" (Luke 22:25–27). It is a reign that does not need to impose its own way on others, for it is sustained by the unseen strength of the righteousness and love of God.

In Luke's version, the prayer for the kingdom leads to the assurance that "the heavenly Father will give the Holy Spirit to those who ask him" (Luke 11:13). This reference to the Holy Spirit appears to be a surprise, since the question is about whether earthly fathers know how to give good gifts. The version in Matthew 7:11 seems more consistent: "Your Father who is in heaven [will] give good things to those who ask him." But Luke is the evangelist who understands the "promise of my Father" (Luke 24:49; Acts 1:4) to be fulfilled in the sending of the Holy Spirit. Indeed this is the beginning of the fulfillment of the restoration of the kingdom to Israel (see Acts 1:6–8; 2).[10]

Not only are the resurrection and exaltation of Jesus a fulfillment of the prayer he taught for the coming of the kingdom but the sending of the Holy Spirit is also God's faithful fulfillment of Jesus' assurance concerning prayer. The kingdom prayer has become a specifically Christian prayer as the evangelist has begun to identify how the exalted Messiah Jesus has become the Lord and Savior whose reign on earth is the answer to the prayer.

AMEN, COME LORD JESUS!

So if the Messiah has come, where is the reign of righteousness and justice and mercy and peace for which suffering humanity was yearning all along? The assurances of the Christian evangelists that the lordship of Jesus is the answer to the kingdom prayer may not easily reassure those who endure outrage and violence and disease and hunger. But because God has vindicated Jesus, who prayed for the kingdom and was executed for enacting its program, the New Testament presentations of the kingdom prayer offer genuine hope. To continue praying for God's kingdom is not an exercise in futility. It is a practice of faith in the God who has raised Jesus from the dead.

The assurance the Gospels offer was not easy, even when their confidence in God was clear. Neither Matthew nor Luke wrote in contexts where Christian triumph was evident. The conflict within the family of Israel was painfully evident in both narratives. Furthermore, neither Matthew nor Luke had any illusions that the kingdom of the Herods or the Roman order could in any way be identified with the reign of Jesus, the true King of the Jews and Savior. To proclaim that Jesus is the Messiah who fulfilled God's promises was certainly no obvious message once the carnage of the Roman siege and destruction of Jerusalem had been completed. The undercaste Christian movement was declaring Jesus to be Messiah, Lord, Son of God, and Savior in the face of harsh evidence that seemed to support the official gospel that Caesar was truly "our Lord and God"—but that was not God's kingdom come on earth.

The Christian prayer for the kingdom is still a plea for God's justice and mercy. It is also a declaration that standing regimes may never arrogate divine authority to themselves. The kingdom prayer will always be a protest against political pretense in the name of the Messiah who was crucified and vindicated by God.[11] But this prayer is also a confession of faith in God, faith that God's apparent foolishness and weakness will not be, cannot be, mocked forever. As Paul put it, "But we impart a secret and hidden wisdom of God, which God decreed before the ages for our glorification. None of the rulers of this age understood this; for if they had, they would not have crucified the Lord of glory" (1 Cor. 2:7–8; see also Acts 4:26–27).

The kingdom prayer rises out of human yearning for a divinely given order of justice. It refuses to relinquish the language of power and dominion even when such words have been used to dominate, because it speaks of a reign where strength is measured in mercy, where authority is exercised in service. As a Christian prayer, it is also grounded in the assurance that God has vindicated the Messiah Jesus and the kingdom he proclaimed, by raising him from the dead. His words and acts reveal the character of God's kingdom on earth. Jesus is God's way of ruling in the world, and faith in Jesus is allegiance to his reign.

Christians have no illusions about the triumph of the reign of the crucified Messiah within the present order. That is why we pray for its coming. But we pray knowing that God has not abandoned this world or us, and we are confident of God's determined will to reign on earth in justice and mercy, as in heaven. In praying for God's kingdom to come and God's will to be done on earth, we call out together, day and night throughout the world, for the presence of God's Holy Spirit and for the full deployment of the reign of God's Messiah Jesus:

> When we cry, "Abba! Father!" it is the Spirit himself bearing witness with our spirit that we are children of God, and if children, then heirs, heirs of God and fellow heirs with Christ, provided we suffer with him in order that we may also be glorified with him. (Rom. 8:15b–17)

NOTES

1. See George Foot Moore, *Judaism*, 3 vols. (Cambridge: Harvard Univ. Press, 1927–30), 2:373.

2. See Jakob J. Petuchowski, "Jewish Prayer Texts of the Rabbinic Period," in *The Lord's Prayer and Jewish Liturgy*, ed. Jakob J. Petuchowski and Michael Brocke (New York: Crossroad, 1978), 21–22, 27.

3. Ibid., 37.

4. Translated portions of the "Hymn to Zeus" are taken from *Hellenistic Religions*, ed. Frederick C. Grant (New York: Bobbs-Merrill, 1963), 152.

5. It may be worth remembering that when Christians use this prayer they still do not conclude with the formula "in Jesus' name." Something of the pre-Christian (pre-Easter) origins of the prayer are still preserved in Christian usage.

6. See Joachim Jeremias, *The Prayers of Jesus*, Studies in Biblical Theology 2/6 (Naperville, Ill.: Alec R. Allenson, 1967); and idem, *The Lord's Prayer*, Facet Books 8 (Philadelphia: Fortress Press, 1964).

7. See Albert Schweitzer, *The Quest of the Historical Jesus*, trans. W. Montgomery, intro. James M. Robinson (New York: Macmillan Co., 1968), 394: "The entry was therefore a Messianic act on the part of Jesus, an action in which His consciousness of His office breaks through. . . . But others can have had no suspicion of the Messianic significance of that which was going on before their eyes. The entry into Jerusalem was therefore Messianic for Jesus, but not Messianic for the people."

8. See Lee E. Snook, "Interpreting Luke's Theodicy for Fearful Christians," *Word and World* 3 (1983): 303–311.

9. See David L. Tiede, *Prophecy and History in Luke-Acts* (Philadelphia: Fortress Press, 1980).

10. See David L. Tiede, "The Exaltation of Jesus and the Restoration of Israel in Acts 1," in *Christians among Jews and Gentiles: Essays in Honor of Krister Stendahl*, ed. George W. E. Nickelsburg and George W. MacRae (Philadelphia: Fortress Press, 1986), 278–86.

11. See Michael H. Crosby, *Thy Will Be Done: Praying the Our Father as Subversive Activity* (Maryknoll, N.Y.: Orbis Books, 1977).

Nine

PRAYER IN PUBLIC LIFE
Paul G. Sonnack

This essay centers on a large question: What does prayer look like when it is practiced in American public life?

The scope of the inquiry has been narrowed to focus on two centers of public life that attract the interest and attention of most Americans: the presidency and the Congress of the United States.[1] The inquiry concludes by looking briefly at the issue of prayer in the public schools of America.

PRAYER AND THE PRESIDENCY

Generally speaking, Americans hold high expectations of the office of the presidency. For one thing, there seems to be a consensus that the president in office bears the responsibility of moral leadership, which is to be exercised by articulating and promoting the supreme values of the nation. Even though there is no obvious agreement on the nature of basic moral issues, it is expected that the president will speak clearly the voice of conscience. On the one hand, he will speak and act in such a fashion as to preserve and protect the established order; on the other, he will function as an agent of social justice by using the immense power of the presidential office to direct American society to goals that are regarded as morally desirable. In one of his major addresses during

121

the campaign of 1968, Richard M. Nixon expressed his awareness of this dimension of the office when he spoke of the possibility of restoring the "moral authority" of the office of president—"to rally the people, to define those moral imperatives which are the cement of a civilized society, to point the ways in which the energies of the people can be enlisted to serve the ideals of the people."[2]

In the view of most Americans, the president in office also plays a unique religious role—and that despite the vaunted partitioning of the religious realm, so-called, from the secular, which is indicated by the phrase "separation of church and state." It is expected that the president will exemplify a civil piety congruent with the religious roots of the nation. It has been claimed that some of the duties of the president are "essentially pastoral."[3] In addition to the president's responsibility of calling the nation to religious celebration by issuing proclamations for annual days of thanksgiving, and of making declarations for the setting-aside of Memorial Day each year as a time for remembrance and prayer, the president is expected to lead the nation in its rites of national triumph and mourning. Beyond that, there is often expressed the general feeling that the president in office will function as an agent of divine guidance for the nation. Many believe that as high priest of a civil religion, he acts in the interest of national unity and well-being.

Though it is expected that the president will be a person of religious faith, there is no specification of what the content of the presidential faith ought to be, nor is there either clarity or consensus as to the ways in which religion should be related to the functions of the office of the presidency. Presumably the religious faith of the president manifests itself in the public arena, at least in covert ways. But essentially it is regarded as a private matter. Americans have learned to accept, perhaps even to expect, from their presidents expressions of a wide diversity of religious opinions and sentiments.

Even a cursory examination of the religion of the presidents indicates that they have held a multiplicity of religious views.[4] The presidents who were instrumental in giving shape to the American republic, George Washington and Thomas Jefferson, were intensely interested in religion but gave expressions to their convictions only in terms of certain Deistic affirmations.[5] Abraham Lincoln, who dedicated himself to the cause of preserving the union, never professed faith in any Christian creed and never joined any church, but he had a profound faith that God, the "Great Disposer of Events," had his own purposes in human history which despite human perversity and the pride of human achievement (as he saw it manifest in both North and South) would ultimately prevail.[6] Woodrow Wilson, who hoped that under his leadership the United States and the League of Nations would become instruments of a just peace, was a staunch Presbyterian who believed that God had selected him to serve the cause of righteousness in the world.[7] Dwight D. Eisenhower, who joined the Presbyterian church after his inauguration, espoused a vague religiosity that bore some resemblance to the old-time religion of the American revival tradition. William Lee Miller observed that Eisenhower was a "very fervent believer in a very vague religion."[8] John Fitzgerald Kennedy was a practicing Roman Catholic, the first to occupy the oval office. According to those who worked closely with him, Kennedy was almost totally uninterested in theology and in the internal affairs of the church.[9] He regarded his faith as a private matter derived not so much from institutional form as from the complex fabric of human experience.[10] Nixon, nominally a Quaker, combined in his faith some survivals of a Protestant moralism with his resounding affirmation of the American dream.[11] Jimmy Carter was a professed evangelical, born-again Christian who manifested a "strong concern for the moral dimension of public policy."[12]

It is clear that the pluralistic character of the religious situation in the United States is reflected in the diversity of religious views that American presidents have held. It is also clear that such views have usually been relegated to what has come widely to be named the area of private religion. With a few notable exceptions (Wilson and Lincoln come especially to mind), there is little indication that the private religion of the presidents has been of much consequence in the conduct of their responsibilities in the public realm. If there has been any religious context for the public functioning of presidents in office, it seems to have been a powerful but ill-defined and constantly shifting consensus consisting of a wide variety of ideological, mythical, and metaphorical components lifted out of the matrix of the American experience.

But what of the presidents and prayer? The record indicates at least two things: (a) that it has not been at all uncommon for American presidents to speak approvingly of prayer and even to commend the practice of prayer to citizens of the nation (some presidents have even indicated that they were themselves persons who prayed); and (b) that there is virtually no indication that presidents in execution of the public responsibilities of their office have spoken public prayers, and that, therefore, with only a few exceptions, there is no record of the prayers of the presidents. It is important for our purposes to give attention to each of these considerations. We shall do so by selecting for brief notice the attitudes and convictions of several American presidents.

From Washington to Ronald Reagan, most presidents have spoken favorably of prayer, have commended it to others, and have sometimes themselves claimed to be persons of prayer. A host of legends about Washington as a man of prayer have as their main source the first biography written by Parson Weems.[13] Although it seems clear that such legends are unreliable, there are strong indications that Washington did regard prayer as important.[14] As soon as he was appointed commander in chief of the Continental army, for example, he took steps to provide chaplains so that prayers could be offered for the "blessing and protection of heaven," particularly necessary "in times of public distress and danger."[15] Moreover, Washington, as general, ordered the observance of special days of "fasting, humiliation, and prayer" in order to "prosper our arms."[16] Again and again in the course of war he encouraged prayers to Divine Providence for assistance in battle, and he seemed to believe that such appeals played a major role in the progress of the American cause. When the war ended, he directed that "thanks to Almighty God for all his mercies" be given, "particularly for his . . . causing the rage of war to cease among the nations."[17] When he assumed the presidency, he indicated in his first inaugural address his sense of the need for the guidance of Divine Providence. Hence, as he put it, he looked to "that Almighty Being . . . who presides in the councils of nations and whose providential aids can supply every human defect."[18] While he was president, he issued thanksgiving proclamations on two separate occasions, in which he called upon all citizens to offer prayers for the mercies bestowed on the new American nation. Quite often in the letters he addressed to religious organizations, Washington indicated that he was praying for their happiness and well-being.[19]

In the opinion of William J. Wolf, who has written the best analysis of Lincoln's religion, Lincoln was "unquestionably our most religious president."[20] As was the case with Washington, a number of legends

have accumulated around Lincoln as a man of prayer.[21] More reliable
reports indicate that Lincoln did speak openly about prayer and that it
became increasingly a source of consolation and strength to him. In a
letter to J. A. Reed in December 1878, Noah Brooks, who was one of
Lincoln's personal acquaintances, wrote, "He said that after he went to
the White House, he kept up the habit of daily prayer. Sometimes it
was only ten words, but those ten words he had."[22] Wolf reports what
John Nicolay, one of Lincoln's secretaries, wrote, "Mr. Lincoln was a
praying man. I know that to be a fact and I have heard him request people to pray for him. . . . I have heard him say that he prayed."[23] Further
evidence of Lincoln's commitment to prayer is to be found in his calls
to public penitence, fasting, prayer, and thanksgiving. He issued nine
calls in the forty-nine months he served as president.[24] Since the time
of Lincoln, American presidents have routinely issued annual calls for
days of national prayer and thanksgiving.

When he was elected president in 1952, Eisenhower declared, "Our
government makes no sense unless it is founded in a deeply felt religious faith, and I don't care what it is."[25] The nation was experiencing
one of its periodical revivals of religion in the 1950s, but most Americans were content with a vague religiosity that, according to Will
Herberg, was "quite peripheral to their everyday lives."[26] Billy Graham was confident that "the overwhelming majority of the American
people felt a little more secure realizing that we have a man who believes in prayer at the helm of our government at this crucial hour."[27]
In 1953, shortly after he became president, Eisenhower helped to inaugurate the White House prayer breakfast. He made an attempt to
establish a national day of prayer. He opened his cabinet meetings
with prayer. Most Americans were persuaded that their president
was a man of prayer.

The first Roman Catholic to be elected president of the United
States, Kennedy made it clear in the heated campaign that preceded
his election that he was fully committed to religious neutrality in the
public realm and that religious sectarianism was to him intolerable.
There are indications that in his private life he continued to receive the
ministrations of his church, but he was scrupulous in avoiding any display of piety either in public or in private. One of his closest confidants
wrote of him, "Not once in eleven years . . . did he ever discuss his personal views on man's relation to God. . . . I never heard him pray aloud

in the presence of others."[28] In the campaign that preceded his election
in 1976, Carter made clear his own personal religious convictions, including his devotion to the practice of prayer. In an interview by the
National Religious Broadcasters on October 14, 1976, Carter was
asked if Bible reading and prayer were essential to him, particularly in
times of crisis. He responded, "Yes, I pray many times during the day,
[especially] when I'm faced with a responsibility that might affect others' lives. I pray as a routine thing. . . ."[29] When he became president,
Carter continued periodically to teach Bible classes in the Plains Baptist Church and at the First Baptist Church in Washington, D.C. Usually he opened and closed these sessions with a free prayer.[30]

The foregoing survey makes it evident that a number of American
presidents have practiced prayer in their private lives, have encouraged others to pray for the welfare of the nation, and have from time to
time issued proclamations calling the entire nation to times of prayer
and thanksgiving.

Given the favorable attitude of presidents toward prayer, it is both
surprising and somewhat puzzling that in the public exercise of the office there is virtually no indication that the presidents prayed at all.
There are only a couple of exceptions to this. Shortly before the inauguration ceremony began, Eisenhower composed a prayer that he
read, after the swearing-in ceremony, as introductory to the inaugural
address.[31] And in November 1977, Carter gave a public prayer at a special service for peace at the First Baptist Church in the capital.[32] This
prayer is not included in the record of the official acts of President
Carter because it has not been thought that he offered it in discharge of
his official duties and responsibilities as president. He offered the
prayer not as president but as a private citizen who happened to be
president of the United States.

Lincoln and Carter were persons who, according to their own public
statements, did practice prayer. Hence one would expect to find some
record of their public prayers. But such is not the case. One searches
the collected writings of Lincoln in vain for a copy of even a single
prayer that he prayed in public. Carter was explicit, even profusely so,
in his endorsement of prayer and in his public indications that he was a
man of prayer. Yet there is no record anywhere of his praying in the
public exercise of the presidential office. In the essays he wrote for distribution in the campaign for the presidency, there is no reference to

prayer.[33] Even more surprising is the fact that in the published memoirs of his term in office (interestingly enough, entitled *Keeping Faith*), there is no mention of prayer.[34]

How is this particular circumstance to be understood? It seems clear that American presidents by and large have approved of religion, have regarded it as important for the being and well-being of the nation and of its individual citizens, and have themselves while in office practiced a form of religion. Moreover, they have approved of prayer and called for its practice; a number of them have in fact professed themselves to be men of prayer. Why, then, has there been a persistent disinclination to offer prayers in public? The answer to that question is probably to be located in the general conviction, largely unspoken, that religion, and especially prayer—which is widely regarded as its most intimate expression—are essentially and deeply personal, hence private and individualistic in character. If the president were to offer prayer in the exercise of his public office, he would violate both the public character of his office and the private character of his religion. And he would infringe upon the fundamental right of religious freedom by threatening the pluralistic character of the American polity.

PRAYER AND THE CONGRESS

Since the beginning of the federal republic, the government of the United States has employed chaplains for both houses of the United States Congress. Each daily session in both houses commences with a prayer by the chaplain.[35] The practice seems at least to imply an acknowledgment that the legislative business of the federal government requires divine guidance and support.[36] A relatively generous sampling of these prayers yields a number of impressions. In form, almost all the prayers seem to be Christian—even Protestant Christian—in orientation. A great many of the allusions made and much of the imagery employed would be familiar to worshiping members of a Christian congregation. There are references, for example, to the "wounded feet of that Master of Men" (Senate, March 10, 1943; citations of the prayers will be made simply by indicating the provenience of each prayer, i.e., Senate or House, and the date of its original presentation), the "pure soul of man's Best Man" (Senate, April 6, 1943), the "blessings which the Saviour has promised us" (Senate, March 4, 1904).

Moreover, the prayers are almost invariably made in the name of Jesus: "in the dear Redeemer's name" (Senate, March 10, 1943), "in his name who was love incarnate" (Senate, January 3, 1985). One of the more extreme examples of this form of address was recently offered in a prayer in the House of Representatives:

> Our most gracious Heavenly Father, it is by the blood of Jesus and on the grounds of Calvary that we come to You today. (House, June 22, 1983)

The prayers sometimes bear ascriptions of praise: "Thy name be praised for the length, the breadth, and the intensity of divine love" (House, October 2, 1945). Occasionally, the prayers make confession, sometimes of sin, mostly of certain defects:

> We know that we have offended Thee by some of the things we have done. We know that Thou canst not bless all that we undertake and dost not approve of all our attitudes. (Senate, December 8, 1947; see also Senate, February 1, 1904)

Quite often the prayers contain intercessions for the president, for members of the Congress, for persons in the military forces of the country (especially in wartime), for all sorts and conditions of people (especially the needy, the infirm, the suffering, the aged), for homes and families, parents and children (Senate, February 11, 1904; Senate, March 17, 1904; House, January 9, 1945). Many of these prayers are individualistic in their orientation, but in some of the prayers there is also manifest a genuine concern for the common good—sometimes expressed with uncommon eloquence:

> In this anguished day of the world's passion and pain, we would purge our own hearts as we face the high demands of the public good committed to our keeping. . . . O Thou Strong Father of the nations, draw all Thy great family together with an increasing sense of our common blood and destiny, that peace and justice, with equal worth and freedom to all, may come at last to a cleansed earth—the home of a holy brotherhood of peoples. (Senate, November 18, 1943; see also Senate, January 11, 1944)

These prayers are filled with petition. The petitioners ask for unity and justice and peace:

> . . . erase from the brow of America the stigma of disunity and give us the will to stand with unyielding conviction for the rule of right and justice. (House, November 5, 1945)

A major burden of most of the prayers of petition is to request divine support and guidance for those exertions of ability and effort which will hold human life on a firm foundation:

> Give us hearts and minds big enough for those social reconstructions . . . that shall yet turn human life into a glad, gracious, and triumphant fraternity around this torn and tortured world. (Senate, November 18, 1942)

Without exception, the prayers offered by the chaplains affirm the nation. They reinforce and deepen the fundamental belief in the mission and destiny of America:

> Lord God of heaven, . . . make America Thy great servant, Thy chosen channel of blessing to all lands. . . . Make this God's own country by making it willing to live like God's people. (Senate, March 3, 1947; see also Peter Marshall's prayers in the Senate delivered January 22, February 11, March 19, March 21, March 27, April 18, and May 2, 1947)

During World War II, Dr. Frederick Brown Harris served as chaplain to the Senate. Again and again in his prayers, the note of America's mission and destiny under God was struck:

> For our country we pray. . . . Help her to heal the open sores of the world, which hate and selfishness and misunderstanding have inflicted on the bleeding body of our common humanity. (Senate, May 5, 1943)

The same theme persists in more recent prayers:

> O Lord, we humbly ask for Your strength to fulfill our destiny with competent, courageous leadership for the betterment of our country and all humankind. (House, May 20, 1986)

A study of these prayers leads to three general observations. First of all, there is the air of generality that pervades them. Only occasionally does a particular prayer reflect the fact that it emerges from and is addressed to a particular historical situation. Most of the prayers would be completely interchangeable—suitable for use in virtually any time and place. There is a sameness to the prayers, and the language employed is routinely platitudinous. Over and again there are prayers for wisdom and justice and peace and righteousness which are only seldom related to the particularities of a situation. The prayers become specific only when they speak of America, and America is almost always lauded as the special object of divine guidance.

Second, the mode and tone of the prayers tend to be individualistic. Obviously they are so in the sense that they are prepared and presented by an individual person and that they reflect, therefore, the commitments and perspectives of that person. One gets the impression that these prayers are being delivered *to* senators and representatives more than that they represent the collective aspirations, sentiments, and perspectives *of* the members. This helps us understand why there is no obvious objection to the Christian forms in which the prayers are couched. The chaplain as an individual prays to God in the presence of the members of the House and Senate; he does not offer prayer as a corporate expression on their behalf. If he articulates the affirmations and petitions of the legislators, it will only be because he has been able to reflect the sentiments of individual persons in his own words. It is expected, therefore, that the chaplain will pray in the manner customary and congenial to him.

Finally, the prayers seem to be largely instrumental in their intention. Hence the predominance of prayer as petition. Only rarely, and then sparely, do the prayers exhibit elements of adoration, praise, and thanksgiving. What confession there is consists mostly of a recitation of weaknesses, mistakes, defects—not of sin. And confession as an affirmation of faith centers on those generalities constituting the American consensus. Prayer is essentially a mode of enlisting divine assistance for the achievement of specific ends, and those ends are understood as fulfilling the purposes of legislators and, more generally, of the American government. There are, therefore, numerous requests for the gifts of wisdom and understanding to the end that good decisions will be made, for courage in the face of oppression and for strength in the place of weakness, for perseverance in the pursuit of righteousness, for stability and order and peace in society, and for discernment in the doing of the justice that will fulfill the promise of America. There is no asking for grace or mercy or love. Nor is there any recognition that the will and purposes of the divine are being subverted as a consequence of the self-righteousness and pride of the American quest for power and that there is need, therefore, to ask for forgiveness and a new beginning.[37] The intent of these public prayers is largely instrumental. Prayer is often regarded as a technique that effects the ends, mostly self-serving, that are regarded as important and valuable for America.

PRAYER IN THE PUBLIC SCHOOLS

Although it is finally of negligible consequence in trying to understand the place of prayer in the public arena, the issue of prayer in the public schools should be discussed briefly.

Throughout most of Western history, it has generally been recognized that there is a close and necessary relationship between religion and education. The teaching of religion has been regarded as providing a necessary basis for morality, which in turn has been deemed essential to the being and well-being of civil society. With the formation of the American republic, the provision for religious freedom written into the federal Constitution (later replicated in many state constitutions) made it mandatory to eliminate divisive sectarian influences from public education. Public education, in the form of the common school, came under the control of the civil state, which was presumed to be neutral in matters of religion. Still the public schools were expected to inculcate into embryo citizens those values and affirmations held together in some sort of consensus. Public schools were to be secular; that is, they were to exclude sectarian particularities, and they were to teach those fundamental affirmations which came to be regarded as the "essentials of all religion."

Beginning in the early years of the twentieth century and continuing into the present, many religious leaders in the United States expressed their concern that public schools were deficient in fulfilling their primary function—as evidenced by the alleged widespread religious illiteracy of American children. Measures had to be devised to overcome this lamentable state of affairs: hence, for example, the experiments in released-time religious instruction and the aggressive efforts to mandate prayer in the routines of each public-school day.

Two instances of the attempt to mandate religious exercises in the public schools became important because the matter of their constitutionality was finally determined in cases before the United States Supreme Court. The first case, *Engel v. Vitale* (1962), came to be known as the Regents prayer case (370 U.S. 421). The Board of Regents of New York's public schools composed a relatively innocuous prayer and urged local school districts to mandate its recitation at the beginning of each school day.[38] The Supreme Court declared the mandated practice unconstitutional on the grounds that it violated the establishment clause of the First Amendment. The second case, *Abington Township School District v. Schempp* (1963; 373 U.S. 203), involved a Maryland law that provided for the recitation of the Lord's Prayer as part of the opening exercises in the public schools of the state. In its decision, the Court invalidated the practice as unconstitutional, again on the grounds that it violated the establishment clause of the First Amendment.

Despite the clear statements of the Supreme Court, efforts continue to be made to put prayer on the agenda of the public-school day. In recent years, there have been proposals, approved and supported in high places, to develop a prayer amendment that would mandate a moment of silence which could be used by students to offer a silent voluntary prayer at the beginning of the school day. It is important to note that the basic issue in all of this has much to say about the interpretation of the religion clauses of the First Amendment but virtually nothing to say about the nature of prayer in the public sector of American life.

It would seem that this study of the phenomenon of prayer in major segments of American public life has made at least two things clear: (*a*) that prayer is much favored, recommended, and employed; but (*b*) that as practiced, it takes on the characteristics of the individualism and instrumentalism that typify much of American public piety.

NOTES

1. There are, indeed, numerous occasions in American life when prayers are offered: e.g., meetings of service organizations, political conventions, and local civic ceremonies, the most prevalent and noteworthy of which has been Memorial Day. Such prayers have not been included in this study, primarily for the reason that there is no record of them.

2. Quoted from Charles P. Henderson, Jr.'s *The Nixon Theology* (New York: Harper & Row, 1972), 24.

3. This was the expressed view of the Rev. Frederick E. Fox, who served as White House chaplain under President Eisenhower. See ibid., 26.

4. See Edmund Fuller and David E. Green, *God in the White House: The Faiths of American Presidents* (New York: Crown Pub., 1968), and Robert S.

Alley, *So Help Me God: Religion and the Presidency, Wilson to Nixon* (Richmond: John Knox Press, 1972).

5. See Paul F. Boller, Jr., *George Washington and Religion* (Dallas: Southern Methodist Univ. Press, 1963); Charles B. Sanford, *The Religious Views of Thomas Jefferson* (Charlottesville: Univ. Press of Virginia, 1984); and Dickinson W. Adams, ed., *Jefferson's Extracts from the Gospels,* The Papers of Thomas Jefferson, 2d ser. (Princeton: Princeton Univ. Press, 1983), intro.

6. See William J. Wolf, *Lincoln's Religion* (Philadelphia and Boston: Pilgrim Press, 1959, and Elton Trueblood, *Abraham Lincoln: Theologian of American Anguish* (New York: Harper & Row, 1973).

7. See John M. Mulder, *Woodrow Wilson: The Years of Preparation* (Princeton: Princeton Univ. Press, 1978).

8. Quoted by Paul Hutchinson in "The President's Religious Faith," *Christian Century* 71 (1954): 367.

9. Theodore Sorenson, *Kennedy* (New York: Harper & Row, 1965), esp. 19.

10. See the discussion of Kennedy in Robert S. Alley's *So Help Me God,* esp. 94–108. See also Albert J. Menendez, *John F. Kennedy: Catholic and Humanist* (Buffalo: Prometheus Books, n.d.).

11. See Charles P. Henderson, *The Nixon Theology,* esp. chap. 10.

12. Richard G. Hutcheson, Jr., "Jimmy Carter's Moral Presidency," *Christian Century* 96 (1979): 1156. See also James T. Baker, *A Southern Baptist in the White House* (Philadelphia: Westminster Press, 1977), and William Lee Miller, *Yankee from Georgia* (New York: Times Books, 1978).

13. See M. L. Weems, *The Life of George Washington* (Frankford [Philadelphia], 1826). See also William J. Johnstone, *How Washington Prayed* (New York, 1932).

14. Most of the information included here has been taken from Boller's *George Washington and Religion,* chaps. 3, 4.

15. Ibid., 52.

16. Ibid., 53.

17. Ibid., 57.

18. Quoted from James Thomas Flexner, *George Washington and the New Nation (1783–1793)* (Boston: Little, Brown & Co. 1969), 185.

19. For copies of the letters Washington sent to religious organizations, see the appendix in Boller's *George Washington and Religion.*

20. Wolf, *Lincoln's Religion,* 192.

21. A compilation of some of the legendary material was made by William J. Johnstone; see his *How Lincoln Prayed* (New York: Abingdon Press, 1931).

22. Quoted from Wolf's *Lincoln's Religion,* 124.

23. Ibid.

24. These calls are to be found in *The Collected Works of Abraham Lincoln,* ed. Roy P. Basler (New Brunswick, N.J.: Rutgers Univ. Press, 1953), vols. 6 and 8.

25. Quoted from Alley's *So Help Me God,* 83.

26. Will Herberg, "Religion and Culture in Present-Day America," in *The Record of American History,* vol. 2, ed. Irwin Unger, David Brody, and Paul Goodman (Waltham, Mass.: Xerox College Pub., 1971), 448.

27. Quoted from William G. McLoughlin, Jr.'s *Billy Graham: Revivalist in a Secular Age* (New York: Ronald Press Co., 1960), 117.

28. Sorenson, *Kennedy,* 19.

29. Quoted from *The Spiritual Journey of Jimmy Carter in His Own Words,* compiled by Wesley G. Pippert (New York: Macmillan Co., 1978), 40.

30. For a sampling of such prayers, see ibid., 46–47.

31. A copy of this prayer is in *Inaugural Addresses of the Presidents of the United States* (Washington, D.C.: U.S. Gov. Printing Office, 1961), 257.

32. A copy of this prayer is in *Jimmy Carter in His Own Words,* 134–36.

33. Jimmy Carter, *Why Not the Best?* (Nashville: Broadman Press, 1975).

34. Jimmy Carter, *Keeping Faith: Memoirs of a President* (New York: Bantam Books, 1982).

35. It is currently the practice to reproduce these prayers in the *Congressional Record.* The decision to do so was made some time after the Civil War. For this study, the *Congressional Record* has been consistently consulted.

36. State legislatures also employ chaplains for the same general purpose. State records have not been consulted for this study.

37. It should be noted that some versions of the American civil religion, and particularly the one proposed by Robert Bellah, understand the primary function of religion to be that of bringing American arrogance and pretension under divine judgment. See Robert N. Bellah, "Civil Religion in America," in *Religion in America,* ed. William G. McLoughlin and Robert N. Bellah (Boston: Houghton Mifflin, 1968), 3–23.

38. The prayer reads, "Almighty God, we acknowledge our dependence upon Thee, and we beg Thy blessings upon us, our parents, our teachers, and our country."

Ten

LEARNING AND TEACHING
PRAYER
Eugene C. Kreider

Teaching prayer begins with the three central objectives of education—thinking, feeling, and acting. Prayer embraces the intellect. It is religious thinking, not because it is qualitatively different from nonreligious thinking but because it is thinking directed toward religion or a religious object, toward whatever one considers divine. Prayer involves the emotions, the world of the senses, wonder, imagination, and those unique personal experiences that are at the heart of religious knowledge. As activity, prayer is expressed in words and signs, gestures, and the capacity to listen.

The objectives for teaching and learning prayer are achieved in both formal and informal settings. In Sunday schools, confirmation classes, adult discussion groups, and other such formal settings, teachers can structure learning and focus it upon specific goals. Objectives are achieved informally in the overall experiences people have in living the Christian life in community with others. The formal way of learning is associated with the classroom and with learning by instruction. The informal way is associated with the process of enculturation or socialization in which one learns the faith by growing up with others who profess it and live it. In both ways of learning the teacher must give attention to the readiness of learners and offer learning experiences appropriate to that readiness by using methods that can adequately communicate the content of learning.

Readiness is a developmental factor involving the mental, emotional, and social development of the learner and the understanding and conceptual ability of the teacher.

When readiness is considered in both classroom learning and enculturation learning, it can receive significantly different emphases. In classroom learning there is a strong emphasis upon the learner's cognitive and affective abilities to receive the learning as structured and directed by the teacher. The learner must be able to *understand*, in the broad sense of that word. In enculturation learning, the emphasis is upon learning through all the experiences one has with others and by gaining an identity or place in the group. Children of all ages can be taught to pray with an emphasis on understanding the words, concepts, and intentions of the prayer. Or children can be taught to pray just by joining in the prayers of others and experiencing the importance of prayerfulness, without understanding the prayers themselves. We shall consider the emphases that readiness can receive, first in terms of the community of prayer and then in terms of understanding prayer.

LEARNERS IN THE COMMUNITY
OF PRAYER

The Christian community is a praying community. It is therefore a community that teaches prayer by its very nature. The community of prayer has a shaping influence on the lives of all its members. Though individuals will experience prayer differently and be at different levels of developmental readiness, everyone learns something about prayer just by being part of the community.

That is because people in a community of prayer have many things in common. They share a common memory and faith that explain the meaning of life under God. They share a vision of who they are and where they are going in images of the kingdom of God. They have a common ritual. They are a pilgrim people who have received a tradition from the past, live it responsibly in the present, and pass it on faithfully to the future.

It is crucial for those who teach prayer in a community of faith for which the Bible is Scripture, to begin with what the biblical record says about prayer and to help believers experience the reality of such prayer in their lives. The appeal to Scripture is not arbitrary. It is confessional. The Bible is profoundly disclosive of what prayer is in the sight of God.

In a community of prayer, people learn many things about prayer through modeling and role taking. Modeling involves living by the examples of others, and role taking involves entering the experiences of others with sympathy and empathy. Moreover, because words are a chief vehicle of prayer, learners need to hear good prayers that come from the tradition of faith, and they need to experience the rhythm of prayer in daily life, the rhythm of praying at the beginning and end of the day, at mealtimes, at work and at play. In these ways people learn the discipline and habit of prayer.

Prayer is constitutive of the life of faith and of the relationship between God and people. It is a way the community teaches about God. Prayer is borne by beliefs about the sovereignty of God, and prayerful living witnesses to beliefs about the relationship of God to humankind. Such beliefs shape the intentions of prayer and the purposes for which people pray. They give prayer its characteristic forms and expressions.

The community of faith is an exposure to prayerful living. One learns there first the importance of prayer, and then the meaning of the words of prayer. The best teaching in the presence of those who do not yet understand prayer is the faithfulness by which it is practiced.[1]

LEARNERS AND UNDERSTANDING PRAYER

When the community of faith takes up the task of helping learners *understand* prayer, the emphasis shifts to the learners' cognitive and affective developmental readiness. Mental, emotional, and social development figure prominently in formal learning settings characterized by classroom instruction.

The objectives for learning in such settings are best achieved with the aid of contemporary studies in the social sciences, especially studies in developmental psychology that owe much to the work of the late Swiss psychologist Jean Piaget.

According to Piaget, learning proceeds in stages or by levels. In early life, learning takes place largely through the senses and intuition. As the mind develops over the years, thinking becomes the ability to put concrete data together in the mind. When mental capacities are fully developed, one is able to think abstractly and propositionally. Learning is a long period of experimentation from childhood to adulthood in which one is constantly trying to make sense out of the world. Planned learning experiences, therefore, must be designed for the learner's stage of development and with a view toward the learner's further growth. Similarly, planned learning experiences must take into account the teacher's ability to form and use concepts necessary for understanding and communicating the content of learning.

After the readiness factor is taken fully into account, the appropriate methods must be selected to convey the content of learning. One needs to let the nature of what is being taught and the objectives sought in the learning process be the determining factors in the selection of methods.

Examples of the way children and adults have understood the Lord's Prayer will illustrate the importance of teaching prayer from the perspective of the learner's readiness. A child of kindergarten age offered this written version of the beginning of the Lord's Prayer: "Our fathe wich are in heaven hallowed by thy name. die king of come die will be done on earth as it is in heaven give us this day of daily breath and forgive us. . . ."[2] Another six-year-old child rendered the first petition of the Lord's Prayer as "Harold be thy name."[3] An adult, while praying this same petition, mused, "I really ought not to use God's name when I swear, I suppose." Or "Thank heaven I don't like some people I could mention."[4]

One cannot assume that the Lord's Prayer is inappropriate for children simply because six-year-old children do not know or understand the concepts and language of the prayer. The problem of both children in the examples was developmental. The prayers of both are illustrations of distortions resulting from verbally conditioned learning without insights into the meaning of the words or phrases. Specifically, the prayer of the second child represents a lack of understanding of the concept of holiness embodied in the word "hallowed." The child used a word from the child's own vocabulary that sounded the same. In both cases the words and concepts were beyond the developmental readiness of the children.

Similarly, one cannot assume that an adult praying this prayer can grasp the meaning of the prayer simply because that person seems to be familiar with the words or phrases. The meaning of the prayer for an adult who is capable of abstract thinking will be influenced very much by the image or concept of God that the adult has in the act of praying. The adult's musing about not using God's name when swearing could easily come from an image of one's relationship to God that is determined by an easygoing familiarity. Such an image finally may or may not be correct. But it seems to miss the dimensions of awe and mystery and holiness that are part of the biblical portrayal of God.

This adult might consider herself or himself ready to teach the Lord's Prayer to children or other people. But the image of God communicated to the learner might not be consistent with the biblical image of God in that prayer. In such a case, one would need to question the teacher's readiness. Teacher readiness means that the teacher must have some awareness not only of her or his own understanding of prayer but also of the way that that understanding corresponds to the meaning of the prayer in its biblical context.

There are several characteristics of people at each stage or level of development that are indicators of conceptual growth or learning readiness and, therefore, helpful guides for the way prayer can be taught. These characteristics are general descriptions that recognize learning readiness as a product of biological and psychological development, of the quality and variety of the environment in which a person experiences life, and of the learning experiences provided by structured educational programs. These characteristics have been developed largely out of the work of Piaget.[5] The characteristics are not absolute descriptions. They do, however, provide a framework through which the teacher can better understand the individual learner.

In discussing these characteristics we shall use three broad groupings: children, teenagers, and adults. In respect to mental development, children are those whose thinking in the early years (ages two to seven) is called preoperational and in later years (ages seven to twelve) is called concrete operational. As children move into their teenage years they begin to develop abstract thinking, which finally characterizes the adult.

The thinking of young children does not make logical connections between things. It centers on individual parts of an experience but does not reason about the relationship of those parts. The thinking of young children is not reversible. Moreover, their vocabulary and their use of words are learned by listening to adults. Children acquire vocabulary much more quickly than an understanding of words and of the ways words are put together meaningfully into sentences.

Fantasy is very important for young children. It is a way they begin to integrate their world and develop simple concepts of reality. Children often use fantasy in talking about their religious worlds. God is visualized in anthropomorphic terms or conceived as unseeable.

The attention span of young children is brief and is usually filled with things that are immediate and uncomplicated. Young children should learn prayer as a simple, brief, uncomplicated expression.

Two characteristics in particular affect the religious development of children in the preoperational period. During this time young children are egocentric and perceptually oriented. Their egocentrism is not premeditated selfishness and should not be judged negatively. Young children cannot take another person's point of view, and they do not seem to care if they are understood or not. Friends are momentary playmates and not lasting companions or people to whom one makes commitments. In addition, whatever children of this age know is limited to what is gained through the senses. The senses perceive, organize, and interpret the data of the young child's world and provide the basis for the inward feelings or emotions. Young children cannot be expected to think about the external world and come to conclusions about it.

It is natural that the prayers of children in their early years should center primarily on themselves. Such prayers should be encouraged and guided so that the way to knowledge through self-knowledge can be utilized to its fullest. Prayers can speak of happiness and sadness, of wanting to be friends, of thankfulness, and the like. After the prayers are said, they are in the past and not objects for lingering experiences and memory or sources for continuing reflection.

Intercessory prayers of young children are not strictly altruistic. Although a child might pray for someone else, such a prayer will probably be governed by egocentrism. Children's prayers for others will reflect a benefit for themselves, expressed or implied. A four-year-old praying for his friend said, "Dear God, please help Johnny *my friend* get well." The prayer for Johnny was really a prayer for Johnny's friendship, which the one praying wanted for himself.

Young children from their early years onward usually think of prayer as efficacious or successful either because they can point to the results of prayer concretely or because they reason from probability, emphasizing convictions or faith.[6]

For the youngest children, prayer is one-way communication. The child speaks to God but is not aware of hearing God. Nor does the child expect God to respond with words. Nevertheless, the child, out of egocentrism rather than faith or trust, knows that prayer brings results. God hears prayers, and results follow. "That's just the way it is," a five-year-old concluded.

For prekindergarten children, prayer is part of their fairy-tale and fantasy experience, in which fairies, Santa Claus, and God are all on the same level. Moreover, what such children think about God comes from their experiences with care givers. Adult modeling is, therefore, very important in these years.

From age seven to age twelve, children's mental capacities develop to the stage of concrete thinking, and their social experiences broaden so that the focus of their lives is no longer primarily the family unit but friends and peer relationships outside the family. These factors of growth influence the way children in this age group understand prayer and the way they pray.

Such children are still limited to what they can know through the senses, but they are beginning to put concrete data together in their minds, understanding logical, cause-and-effect, and sequential relationships.

God, for children in these ages, is still visualized in human form, often as a superhuman who can do all kinds of extraordinary things. The youngest in this group use the names God and Jesus interchangeably and therefore vary the address of prayers without implying different images of the divine.

Children in the preteenage years are discovering their identity in ever-broadening social contexts. As their perception of the world widens, their prayer life becomes more inclusive. Egocentrism gives way to a growing awareness of the needs of others. Prayers can be more altruistic, because these children are gaining the ability to see the point of view of others.[7] Prayers for material gifts, however, are still fairly frequent, and prayers of self-examination are rare.[8]

As people reach their teenage years they gradually acquire the ability to think abstractly and make logical connections between things, seeing the interrelation of parts and the whole. At this stage of thinking, people develop a more spiritual idea of God.

Personal convictions and faith in God become the guides for understanding prayer. Youth begin to understand prayer as a dialogue with God, a two-way communication in which they speak to God and God speaks to them. They recognize that God speaks to people in numerous ways and that therefore prayer always involves listening.

The environment of teenagers changes rapidly, and they are constantly challenged to adjust. Struggles with expectations about life often lead to an uneasy discovery of self and to difficulty in becoming intimate with others and God. And yet the image of God is often that of a personal friend, encouraging intimacy in prayer that can easily lead to an identification with the humanity of Jesus and to prayers addressed to him.

The prayers of teenagers are often the impetus to expressing the inwardness of the religious dimension concretely in the world. In particular, prayers for others are viewed as calling for human action.

Although abstract thinking characterizes the thinking of people from teenage years through adulthood, it does not produce uniformity of experience. It is probably easier to recognize variety in teenagers, because of the physical and social growth they go through, than in adults, whose physical growth is more complete and whose social activities have become more selected and patterned through an increasing awareness of self and others in their world.

Nevertheless, one cannot assume that everyone who has gone through the teenage years and entered adulthood uses abstract thinking in all areas of life. The maturing of one's mind does not mean that one automatically uses mental capacities to their fullest. The capacity to think needs to be exercised. Thinking needs to be practiced. Learners in the faith need help and challenge from others in order to use their maturing mental capacities for better understanding.

That need is especially prominent among many adults when it comes to religious matters, particularly prayer. It is often the case that people drift away from religious nurture in church and home in the early teens, when their thinking about religion is still in the concrete operational stage. Accordingly, they take with them into their adult years ideas about God and prayer and the practice of prayer that have not grown much beyond early adolescence.

TEACHING ABOUT PRAYER AND PRAYING

Teaching about prayer and praying is teaching about a relationship of communication between God and people. It considers the educational readiness of the learner and includes what Scripture, theological and historical reflection, and contemporary cultural materials say about that relationship, along with all the opportunities to learn about prayer informally through experiences in the community of faith. With that in mind, we turn now to methods that can be used to help the learner understand, appreciate, and participate in prayer.

The activity of prayer in words, sighs, and gestures and in the capacity to listen is expressed in different forms that are useful paradigms for teaching prayer. Prayer is *petition,* praying for oneself. It is *intercession,* praying for the needs of others. It is *confession,* repenting of wrongs done and seeking forgiveness. It is *thanksgiving,* offering glory to God. It is *lament,* crying in distress and beseeching God for vindication. It is *praise,* giving honor and adoration to God. These forms provide the occasional structures for prayer. They set the mood for the relationship of prayer, and they govern what is communicated in the activity of prayer.

The teacher is as important as the prayer in the learning process. It is not enough to teach the words of prayer and what they mean. The one who teaches must be a person who prays, a model, so that the practice of prayer can be taught. The richer the prayer experience offered by the teacher in word and example, the richer will be that experience for the learner.

And yet modeling ought not be so personal that it becomes just an example of how one individual prays. Formal and communal prayers as well as spontaneous and private prayers need to be part of the modeling. It is important too that the teacher offer not only herself or himself as a model but also others from the Bible and from the history of the community of faith.

The heritage of prayer in the Christian community is rich in variety.

It brings together all sorts and conditions of human life and historical occasions when people have prayed. It is a witness to the importance of prayer, an encouragement to pray, and an example of the form and content of prayer. It is important, therefore, for teachers to help learners at each age level to become acquainted with this heritage through repeated use of the prayers found there.

Young children to about age seven understand their world from a very personal perspective. In those years, ego growth and expression are dominant, and everything is thought to be as it appears. Planned learnings, including prayer, have to coincide with the learners' experiences.

Because of ego dominance, it is helpful to let children's prayers focus on themselves. Guide children in speaking to God not only with petitions but also with thanksgiving. "Help me, God . . ." and "Thank you, God . . ." prayers allow children to be with God in terms of their experience.

Teachers are often discouraged when young children do not respond to the invitation "Let's fold our hands, bow our heads, and close our eyes." The posture is very difficult for a egocentric child. It is much easier for children to respond to a suggestion for internal constraints, such as "Let's get quiet within ourselves." That kind of suggestion allows the child to be more naturally in control rather than trying to obey external directions.

Because learning is so much by imitation in the early years, the use of set prayers learned by memory can help a child grasp the routine of prayer and the importance of prayer in daily life. Children need the security of routine and can find that security in the act of praying. Caution must be taken, however, to be sure the child understands the meanings of the words of the prayer so that misconceptions do not occur.[9]

Keeping prayers short is important for young children, who cannot easily handle more than one variable at a time. Encourage children to use prayers that are simple and focused. For example, "Thank you, God, for the sunshine" is easier to grasp than "Thank you, God, for the sunshine and all the flowers the sunshine helps grow in my garden." Or "God, I'm sorry" is easier than "God, please forgive me for the things I've done wrong to other people."

Though most prayers of young children are materialistic and egocentric, these children can be encouraged to grow in their prayer life through guidance with intercessory prayers. That guidance should include the challenge to think about how the person prayed for feels. In this way, the child learns to take the point of view of the other person.

As children grow between ages seven and twelve the number and variety of prayers increase. Because of broadening social experiences, children in these years begin to reassess all aspects of religion and faith. They should be encouraged to put their thoughts and feelings about these matters into prayers.

The personal prayer life of the ten- or twelve-year-old needs to be affirmed and supported as the person grows into the early teenage years. In those years it is important for youth to develop a private relationship with God through prayer. Prayers of confession and for reconciliation can flow naturally out of that relationship because of the growing internal, selfhood needs of youth. Because of the challenge of abstract thinking, teenagers continue to wrestle with the question of God's answer to prayer. It is because of this wrestling that youth can be helped to understand that part of prayer is listening to God.

That latter aspect of prayer is important as one lives through adulthood. By the time people reach adulthood, many carry with them the impression that prayer is primarily talking to God, even though they believe God answers prayer. Often for adults the act of praying does not include listening for God to answer. More often than not, people expect God to answer prayer with results in their lives or through some unspecified means, asserting that "things will just turn out all right!" Encouraging quiet times for listening to God is an important aspect of teaching prayer to adults.

Adult prayers need guidance in three other respects. Just as prayers of children need to coincide with life experiences, so adults need to be attentive to their life-cycle needs and let those needs inform their prayers. Second, adults need to be encouraged in the practice of prayer as a way of life and not as a stopgap means of holding life together. Saint Paul's exhortation to prayer constantly gives direction for prayer as a way of life (1 Thess. 5:17). Third, adults need to understand that prayer engenders concepts of God, just as concepts of God engender the life of prayer. Praying is a way toward the knowledge of God.

Learning and teaching prayer is a matter of learning readiness at all ages, the tradition and heritage of faith, and the way those are brought together by the teacher to achieve the objectives of learning. Prayer is not like the involuntary responses of the body. People learn to pray, and that activity involves the whole person, maturing and growing in the presence of God.

NOTES

1. Three books by John H. Westerhoff present the case for enculturation learning: *Bringing Up Children in the Christian Faith* (Minneapolis: Winston Press, 1980); *Building God's People in a Materialistic Society* (New York: Seabury Press, 1983); and *A Pilgrim People: Learning through the Christian Year* (Minneapolis: Seabury Press, 1984).

2. Ronald Goldman, *Readiness for Religion: A Basis for Developmental Religious Education* (New York: Seabury Press, 1970), 81.

3. Ronald Goldman, *Religious Thinking from Childhood to Adolescence* (New York: Seabury Press, 1964), 1.

4. I recall this anecdote from Edmund Steimle's sermon "Prayer's Lost Dimension," preached on "The Protestant Hour" in 1958. I do not have the exact reference.

5. Jean Piaget, *Science of Education and the Psychology of the Child* (New York: Viking Press, 1970). See also idem, *Six Psychological Studies*, trans. Anita Tenzer (London: Univ. of London Press, 1968); and David Elkind, *Children and Adolescents: Interpretive Essays on Jean Piaget*, 3d ed. (New York: Oxford Univ. Press, 1981).

6. Goldman, *Religious Thinking*, 184.

7. Goldman, *Readiness*, 133.

8. Goldman, *Religious Thinking*, 191.

9. Ibid.

How does it all add up? To what have we come? After three years of discussion in the prayer colloquium and beyond, and after these several chapters, where are we? Perhaps it is best to proceed by negation. Where are we? We are not one and we are not done.

We are not one. Someone might say, "They speak with one voice, the voice of white male senior faculty at a midwestern Lutheran seminary." There is no doubt that we lack the angles of vision available to persons writing from and in situations radically different from our own. But even with such continuities as there are among us, we have not really spoken with one voice.

Yet we have affected one another. Each of us now speaks differently of prayer. The conversation probably includes less posturing and speechmaking. There is more listening, more attending to the word of the other. But what is to be heard here is not seamless. Take a matter about which we do agree: that God is known apart from where God is best known, the person and work of Jesus Christ. We speak differently about this. Some will emphasize the mystery and even horror of the hidden God whom one meets apart from Christ. Without God's gracious turning, it is impossible for a mortal to stand before God and live. Others, however, will stress that that gracious turning has occurred already, for God was indeed in Christ "reconciling the *world* to himself" (2 Cor. 5:19). On the basis of that event, they would say that God seeks humankind and hence that people may relate to a gracious God whether they know and can name this gracious God or not. The Christian does claim to know this gracious God decisively, because the Christian knows Jesus.

Perhaps we still speak differently not merely because of who we are. Perhaps we speak differently because our subject defies some final and comprehensive statement. We are speaking of prayer. And of what

does prayer speak? It speaks of our relationship with God, of God's relationship with us. If that is our subject, how should we expect to speak
with one voice? In our worship we use our voices to sing of the One
who is "immortal, invisible, God only wise" and we declare that
"there's a wideness in God's mercy like the wideness of the sea." Of
course, then, we are not one; no one word could compass that width.

Yet there are large convergences and guiding central insights about
the relationship with God. These chapters make clear that we are able
to make some statements together:

- Prayer is a gift from God for human communication with God. It
  is an integral and expected part of the life of faithful individuals
  and communities.
- In giving us a personal name (Yahweh, Jesus), God becomes
  uniquely available to those who faithfully call upon that name.
- Prayer in the name of Jesus is to be consistent with the gospel,
  which has been supremely revealed and embodied in Jesus' life,
  death, and resurrection.
- Prayer is efficacious, but its effects are not finally predictable.
- Prayer is appropriately reflective of all aspects of the faith,
  from matters of creation to those of redemption, sanctification,
  and consummation.

Other statements of convergence could be added. In such statements we are developing the claim that our life and faith take place in
relation to God. Created in God's image, human beings derive both
their existence and their destiny from the Creator. Even in sin we are
not left to ourselves. Beginning with Abraham and Sarah, God has
been about the business of re-creation, redemption, and reconciliation. For Christians all of this is made emphatically clear in God's work
in Jesus Christ. Life itself (John 1:3) and life abundant (John 10:10)
come only through the Word. Both life and faith are seen as gifts. But in
our relationship with God, life and faith, though not our own achieve-
ments, are real for us; they are really given. They are present now, part
of us, enabling us to participate in the relationship. Thus prayer, as our
address to God, is real and efficacious in that relationship as well. We
can pray to God.

As a consciously focused activity, prayer involves our knowing and being known. We can truly know God because God truly knows and is truly related to us. To declare that the relationship with God is crucial is to recognize that we cannot go outside the relationship (as if, say, to know some God alone in solitary splendor) and that we do not need to try to do so. We cannot do so, for our life is truly contained in this relationship. We need not do so, for God is truly present in this relationship. In this relationship we believe that we can know what we need to know about God. This knowledge is a matter of faith and not proof, but it is sufficient to guide and sustain the Christian. The Christian prays in hope, in confident hope. And so we have set about to write with some confidence.

Given our theme, then, it is not so strange that we are not simply one in our speaking. It follows too that we are not done. There is much, much more to be pondered. There are clearly specific topics deserving of study that have gone untreated or barely noted here. For example, we have not treated the understanding of prayer possessed by the Reformers or figuring in the Puritan and pietistic traditions. Insufficient attention has been given to mysticism and to prayer as meditation. The charismatic movement has not been considered. There is much more to be done in the study of prayer.

There is another sense in which we are not done, in which we could never be done. We have offered here Christian thought concerning prayer. But thought and belief do not live off themselves. Belief's brave and bold sentences spring from something far deeper. Our sentences have tried to refer to that, for they have been about our relationship with God. Even those of us who decline to be identified as mystics may recognize that our formulations do not exhaust our relationship with God. We may prefer to speak of our life "before" God instead of our life "in" God. But we can understand from our own experience a mystical testimony to prayer:

> Language falters, . . . language is necessarily complex. It is always moving from expressed meaning to unexpressed, from denotation to connotation. . . . We must go beyond words, confiding ourselves to God, letting God help us lift our hearts to him in silence and sometimes even without images. All of this is particularly clear to us when we reach the upper terraces of prayer; . . . we are well beyond words, yet not outside either thought or feeling. . . . Like the mystics who turn to the images of the Song of Songs, we frequently find that narrative of wooing and sex-

ual union satisfactory. . . . And yet even its exalted measures may be too much, too complicated, too multifaceted and overladen with too many movements away from the central fact: love.[1]

Some of us might not recognize the "upper terraces" as our territory; we might say we are silent—or best silent—out of sheer ineptitude. But we will agree that our pilgrimage as people who pray is not yet complete. Paul, the witness to the blinding Damascan vision, wrote that when the perfect comes the imperfect will pass away (1 Cor. 13:10). And C. S. Lewis, who fashioned many words in defense of Christian faith, closed his "eschatological" novel *Till We Have Faces* with this:

> I ended my first book with the words *no answer.* I know now, Lord, why you utter no answer. You are yourself the answer. Before your face questions die away. What other answer would suffice? Only words, words; to be led out to battle against other words. Long did I hate you, long did I fear you. I might—[2]

We are not now at the then of perfected sight and understanding. We are not done with our Christian pilgrimage and we are not done with our study of prayer. But we believe that we have begun, and this book, exactly a primer, is part of that. With this beginning we make bold to continue. And it is not only the study of prayer which is unfinished. There is also the praying.

NOTES

1. Ann and Barry Ulanov, *Primary Speech: A Psychology of Prayer* (Atlanta: John Knox Press, 1982), 124–25.
2. C. S. Lewis, *Till We Have Faces* (Grand Rapids: Wm. B. Eerdmans, 1977), 308.

Selected Bibliography

Anderson, Bernhard W. *Out of the Depths: The Psalms Speak for Us Today*. Philadelphia: Westminster Press, 1983. An introduction to the psalms according to literary type. Anderson deliberately addresses contemporary theological issues and writes for the general reader.

Baelz, Peter. *Prayer and Providence*. New York: Seabury Press, 1968. An effort to guide us toward a synthesis of God's universal providential working and God's personal responding to particular prayers.

Bonhoeffer, Dietrich. *Psalms: The Prayer Book of the Bible*. Minneapolis: Augsburg Pub. House, 1970. An unabashedly christocentric devotional view of the Psalter. For Bonhoeffer, the psalms became our prayers because they were the prayers of Jesus.

Cragg, Kenneth. *Alive to God: Muslim and Christian Prayer*. London: Oxford Univ. Press, 1970. A collection of a wide variety of both Muslim and Christian prayers, with a sensitive introduction that is vintage Cragg— theologian and Islamist.

Cunningham, Agnes, s.s.c.m. *Prayer: Personal and Liturgical*. Message of the Fathers of the Church 16. Wilmington, Del.: Michael Glazier, 1985.

Fisher, Fred L. *Prayer in the New Testament*. Philadelphia: Westminster Press, 1964. One of the best introductions to prayer in the New Testament. The book covers a wide range of topics, including the theology of prayer in the New Testament, the forms of prayer that appear there, effective prayer, bodily postures, the wording of prayers, and much more.

Hargreaves, John H. M. *A Guide to Psalms*. TEF Study Guide 6. London: SPCK, 1973. An attempt by the former warden of Buwalasi College, in Uganda, to relate the psalms to the lives of people in the Third World. In the process, the book provides new insights into the meaning and use of the psalms for all readers.

McFadyen, John E. *The Prayers of the Bible*. London: Hodder & Stoughton, 1906. A rich resource for the study of prayer in the Bible. Long out of print, this book takes up such topics as the themes of prayer in the Bible and the relation of faith and prayer, and it provides an anthology of the prayers of the Old Testament and the New Testament under various categories (petition, intercession, thanksgiving, etc.).

Mbiti, John S. *The Prayers of African Religion*. Maryknoll, N.Y.: Orbis Books, 1975. A collection of many African prayers, by a well-known African theo-

151

logian who provides a general introduction as well as sectional
introductions.

Minister's Prayer Book. Edited by John W. Doberstein. Philadelphia: Fortress
Press, 1986. A classic resource for devotion, in the opinion of many. Published in 1959, this prayer book has been reprinted in response to popular
demand. It contains orders of prayer for morning, noon, and evening each
day of the week. Over three hundred prayers and more than three hundred readings for meditation are included. These come from virtually
every era of church history. Most have to do with the life and ministry of
the parish pastor.

Oxford Book of Prayer. Edited by George Appleton. New York: Oxford Univ.
Press, 1985. A large collection of prayers from the Bible, Christian history,
and other traditions of faith.

Petuchowski, Jakob J., and Michael Brocke. *The Lord's Prayer and Jewish Liturgy.* New York: Crossroad, 1978. A collection of essays that is especially
valuable for placing the Lord's Prayer within the prayer traditions of Israel
without always using other Jewish prayers as negative comparisons.

Westerhoff, John H. *Bringing Up Children in the Christian Faith.* Minneapolis:
Winston Press, 1980. A view of faith as the perception and awareness of the
grace of God. In this book Westerhoff talks about the ways in which faith is
nurtured in the Christian community.

Wilson, John F. *Public Religion in American Culture.* Philadelphia: Temple
Univ. Press, 1979. An indispensable discussion of religious phenomena
that pervade American culture and that are expressed in the common, public arena.